I'm so glad we met,

Lii

EMPLOYEE GROUP BENEFIT
INSIGHT
An Informal Reference Guide

LORI POWER

Copyright © 2018 Lori Power.

All rights reserved. No part of this book may be used or reproduced by any means, graphic, electronic, or mechanical, including photocopying, recording, taping or by any information storage retrieval system without the written permission of the author except in the case of brief quotations embodied in critical articles and reviews.

Archway Publishing books may be ordered through booksellers or by contacting:

Archway Publishing
1663 Liberty Drive
Bloomington, IN 47403
www.archwaypublishing.com
1 (888) 242-5904

Because of the dynamic nature of the Internet, any web addresses or links contained in this book may have changed since publication and may no longer be valid. The views expressed in this work are solely those of the author and do not necessarily reflect the views of the publisher, and the publisher hereby disclaims any responsibility for them.

Any people depicted in stock imagery provided by Thinkstock are models, and such images are being used for illustrative purposes only.
Certain stock imagery © Thinkstock.

ISBN: 978-1-4808-5635-6 (sc)
ISBN: 978-1-4808-5636-3 (e)

Library of Congress Control Number: 2018900103

Print information available on the last page.

Archway Publishing rev. date: 01/31/2018

DISCLAIMER

The following are blog postings. This is not a peer-reviewed journal, a sponsored publication or the product of editing. While the ideas and thoughts are often vital, pertinent and relevant to the employee group benefit marketplace in Canada, specifically Alberta, the views and opinions represented are just that—opinions—and they belong solely to the blog author and do not represent those of people, institutions or organizations the author may or may not be associated with in a professional or personal capacity, unless explicitly stated. The views and opinions are not intended to malign any religion, ethnic group, club, organization, company or individual.

In no particular order, all content provided is for informational purposes only. The author makes no representations as to the accuracy or completeness of any information found by following any links. The author will not be liable for any errors or omissions in this information or for the availability of this information. The author will not be liable for any losses, injuries or damages from the display or use of this information.

Websites are filled with dynamic content but don't enable conversations, while blogs do.

Blog content, by design, is dynamic. The contents of a blog today may in fact change over time, including the blog author's opinion.

The blog author is not responsible or liable for anything anyone says in the comments. Because blogs are global, note comments in blogs are based on Canadian content unless referenced otherwise.

CONTENTS

Section 1: Why Benefits?
Choice and Solutions 1

Section 2: Price Matters
The Compensation Strategy
Dollars and Sense 13

Section 3: Plan Design
Building Compensation 57

Section 4: The End User
All about the Employee 89

Section 5: Employee Death Benefits
Replacement of Salary 143

Section 6: Experience Rated Benefits
Pharmacy
Extended Health Care
Vision Care
Dental Care
Employee Assistance
Health Spending Accounts
Administrative Services Only 187

Section 7: The Pillars of Business
Who Pays the Bill 237

Section 8: Why Use a Broker?
Working with an Expert 261

Section 9: Just 'Cause 297

INTRODUCTION

As an informal reference, the content is all about education and communication—customer service.

As I pull this book together, it is unlikely I'll tell readers anything they don't already know. As a benefits broker, I am not unique, but I am earnest and try every day to provide my customers with exceptional service and be there for them as though each were my only client. I have found over the years that the best way to understand insurance and insured products is through the real-life stories of how having or lacking insurance impacts the end user.

This book contains a compilation of insurance industry scenarios told through real events experienced by real clients in various scenarios.

Section 1
 Why Benefits?
 Choice and Solutions

Section 2
 Price Matters
 The Compensation Strategy
 Dollars and Sense

Section 3
 Plan Design
 Building Compensation

Section 4
 The End User
 All about the Employee

Section 5
    Employee Death Benefits
    Protection of Income

Section 6
    Prescription Drugs
    Extended Health Care
    Vision Care
    Dental Care
    Employee Assistance Program
    Emergency Medical Assistance
    Administrative Services Only
    Health Spending Accounts

Section 7
    The Pillars of Business
    Who Pays the Bill

Section 8
    Why Use a Broker?
    Working with an Expert

Section 9
    Just 'Cause

Remember that insurance is subject to change, as insured contracts amend and political parties alter the rules, and blog postings are at the mercy of when they were written. However, I am confident the basics and majority of discussions will stand the test of time. It is my fondest hope that reading these entries as an employer or decision maker, human resources professional or plan administrator will make your job easier.

Kindest regards,
Lori Power, GBA, exclusively specializing in employee group benefits

Section 1

Why Benefits?
Choice and Solutions

WHY BENEFITS?

When Should an Employer Consider Adding a Benefit Plan?

John Employer owns a small business. He pays competitive wages and provides good working conditions. It takes several weeks and many hours of his time to train a new employee.

He finds it difficult, though, to keep some staff for more than a year or so. John is upset that some move on to work for a competitor. He has had trouble attracting and retaining someone who can handle the key position of assistant manager. John wonders if there is a better way to attract and keep quality people—build a compensation package.

A good salary is certainly high on any employee's list of reasons to stay with an employer, but work-life balance matters, and staff are also concerned about what happens when they get sick or hurt, need dental work or perhaps die.

Group employee benefits might be the answer to control costly staff turnover. Typically, a group plan will provide all employees, regardless of an existing health condition, with life insurance, disability protection, extended health-care benefits and dental coverage. A group retirement plan can also be part of the package.

Both the employer and the employee generally share the cost of a group plan. If an employee pays entirely for certain benefits, such as disability insurance, any benefits received as a claim are tax free. Employee contributions to a retirement plan are tax deductible.

By implementing a group plan, John can compare with his competition by attracting and keeping top-notch employees. All of his costs in providing the plan are tax deductible to the corporation.

ADVANTAGES OF BENEFITS

Twenty Advantages of Employee Group Benefits

1. As many employees do not own a life policy that is not connected to a mortgage or a loan, sometimes the only insurance they have is through their employer.
2. Life insurance provides a corporate policy in the event of an employee's death.
3. An accidental death and dismemberment benefit provides a lump-sum payment to ease changes in lifestyles as well as unexpected deaths.
4. Disability coverage initiates a corporate policy in the event of an injury or illness. What is the corporate policy in the event of a disability of a valued, long-standing employee?
5. A group policy, without medical evidence being required in most instances, provides for 24-hour coverage for all benefits, including disability insurance.
6. It provides out-of-country emergency care for business or pleasure, so the need for individual travel insurance is reduced and often eliminated.
7. Drug coverage is available, without undue restrictions, by submission of receipts or through pay-direct drug cards.
8. Employee assistance programs provide 24-hour counseling services.
9. Health and dental coverage for day-to-day expenditures helps keep a family healthy.
10. Conversion privileges are available for both life and disability products.

11. It provides a tax-deductible alternative to a raise in pay.
12. Benefits are less expensive than a raise, because there are no additional increases in CPP, EI or WCB payments.
13. Benefits help attract and retain key employees.
14. They increase productivity and the quality of employees' work.
15. Healthier employees reduce turnover and absenteeism.
16. Group insurance is an investment in a company's well-being rather than an expense.
17. Benefits increase morale and give the company a leg up over the competition.
18. There are no in-the-box plans. Custom-designed benefits specifically tailored to corporate needs assist in achieving corporate goals and objectives.
19. Employees and employers receive benefits without having to belong to associations, which usually require membership fees.
20. Employees and their families are protected against devastating and catastrophic events.

MULTIPLE PRODUCTS

Benefits Are Not Just One Product

Ushering change for small business owners for almost 20 years means proudly offering innovative benefits solutions employees want at prices employers can afford.

What Could Be Better Than Great Coverage at a Tremendous Value?

Even two decades ago, many products now considered commonplace to small businesses owners were only available to large companies. I remember distinctly the day my outlook on benefits changed. I was presenting a renewal to a client and walked in elated I had negotiated reduced rates. Should have been an easy meeting, right?

Wrong.

The client was upset, and here was his reasoning:

Each year, the broker showed up around September to present the renewal. The company year-end was completed in August after he had spent the summer planning his budget. Good or bad, the timing of the renewal meant the new numbers threw off the financial plan.

His words to me were "I need something where I can predict from one year to the next what my costs will be. I need a plan where I can budget a certain percentage per employee for the benefit cost in the same manner I budget all other aspects of my business."

Only by listening to employers can we actually build what they need.

This event changed not only the way I viewed benefits but also how I implemented and designed plans for all future clients. And he was right. Benefits have to mirror the compensation strategy and their business strategy, regardless of size. While we should never place a plan strictly based on price, budgets matter.

Make benefits a foundational tool for the company.

In addition to finding specialized providers able to offer health spending accounts to small businesses, I endeavored to remove the "complicated" from insurance. This means if coverage is intended and everyone understands something should be claimable, then it should be covered. We should have none of this least cost alternative pricing where employees go to the counter assuming coverage, only to be told the prescription they were prescribed doesn't fall within the coverage parameters. I hate just the thought of that, as I can only imagine the frustration that would cause me if I needed a script for one of my kids. Come on—consider if all who read the employee booklet think they're covered at 100 percent for basic dental services and only find out when they are preparing to leave the dental office that—oops—due to dental fee guide restrictions, they are actually only getting reimbursed at 70 percent. No one wins in that scenario.

Speaking of claims, the process doesn't have to be hard or complicated. Ease of claims processing is essential. This would include the use of smartphone applications, claiming via the web, point of service, using a credit card platform, photo claims and, of course, the old-fashioned paper route.

On this note, plan members and administrators can log on to web-enabled portals to review coverage details, set up direct deposit and make administrative changes in real time. These easy-to-use platforms ensure members have everything they need to manage their accounts anytime, anywhere.

If you haven't yet given benefits a chance or you have a plan that has not been built to suit the specific needs of your company, consider what you want for your employees, and allow a specialized broker to build it within budget. This would include but is not limited to the following:

- Life insurance
- Accidental death and dismemberment
- Dependent life
- Short-term disability
- Long-term disability
- Critical illness
- Extended health care
- Pharmacy
- Professional services
- Employee assistance
- Travel insurance
- Vision care
- Dental care
- Major restorative
- Orthodontics
- Administrative services only
- Health spending accounts
- Group RRSP
- Pension plans

Always build to suit!

OFFERING A GROUP BENEFIT PLAN

Reasons to Implement Benefits

Despite the goodwill to employees, ultimately, the tax savings is the number-one reason to implement a benefit plan.

The protection of the corporation's most valuable asset—the employees—is the result of implementing a strategic benefit plan with options.

The reason is because employees who enjoy peace of mind in a financial safety net are better able to concentrate on what the company hired them to do: make money.

Employee assistance plans allow employees to access the services required to get them through home-life stresses without embarking on coworker psychology sessions, which cause the loss of two people from the workforce for the duration of this issue.

When it comes to life and disability benefits, employers often offer an employee group benefit plan out of a sense of obligation to protect their employees. However, this thought can be turned around, and a benefit plan can actually offer protection for the employer. Life and disability saves the company time, energy and, most importantly, money when an employee has a need. With this coverage in place, the employer has no financial obligation to the employee or his or her beneficiaries other than what the coverage states.

It happens—diagnosis of unmentionable illnesses and conditions people fear: cancer, heart attack, stroke, disease, paralysis, blindness and the list goes on. Critical illness and remote expert second opinion options on a benefit plan could mean the difference between a life cut short but not cut off and a life well lived. This coverage is not only affordable but also becoming increasingly necessary in any professional work environment.

Health spending accounts are an emerging trend in benefits. As a business, staying competitive and remaining competitive in the marketplace mean having a superior benefit plan. This is where offering items outside the norm will attract top talent. What would it mean to employees to choose where they spend their allocated benefit dollars?

Health and dental benefits are offered tax free on plans outside the province of Quebec. The value of before-tax expenses can mean as much as a 30 percent savings to employees. Consider this: How much would individuals have to earn to pay for a $100 dental bill? The answer relies on the tax bracket. If they are in a 32 percent tax bracket, then they would need to earn $132 to pay for that $100 bill. How valuable is an employee group benefit plan if that $100 is covered under the benefit plan? Tax free. Now we have just added to the employee's compensation in a positive fashion.

A well-designed employee group benefit package should reflect the company's business strategy and overall compensation platform.

Group Quotations

Looking to implement coverage? Don't treat it like a commodity.

Don't be daunted by the complications and rules of insured benefits.

Remember, employee group insurance is a *group* of individual insurance products *grouped* together for a *group* of individuals financially linked through common employment.

Insurance providers are a shrinking market, so the first item of business is to choose a broker—someone who will listen to what you need and then gather various quotations from different insurance companies and analyze the information accordingly. Remember, insurance carriers (Manulife, Sun Life, Great-West Life, Standard Life, RBC Insurance, etc.) will release only one quote to one broker. For another broker to receive a quote on the same client, the original broker must, in essence, be fired from the case. Traditionally, this is done through an agent of record letter, which is a letter of engagement.

Note that a broker is not bound by any one insurance company. Brokers are their own companies and work for the client—always.

An insurance agent, on the other hand, is bound to one insurance company and works for that company only. A client may deal with an agent of that company, but that agent will always be biased toward the insurance company that pays him or her.

Benefit brokers apply strategies to achieve solutions by listening to the wants and needs of the employer group. This will typically involve an analysis of the existing benefit plan (if available) to get a real feel for what is going on with that benefit plan that has caused the client to seek alternate quotations. The broker gets to know what the company is paying for, what has been used and what is not used or valued by the employees.

The next step is to develop and build a plan design that will be able to be modified for that client as they grow and change as a business.

Then and only then will the broker canvass the marketplace for pricing on benefits, and by that point, all are clear about the objectives of what they want to achieve with the benefit plan as an overall business solution.

Insurance can be complicated by those who like to be complicated—but it doesn't have to be.

We like simple, straightforward solutions that work for our clients in attaining their benefit goals.

Section 2

Price Matters
The Compensation Strategy
Dollars and Sense

TAX AND BENEFITS

Always consult your accountant for accurate tax information.

A Simplified View of Government Policy on Taxation of Employee Benefits

Employee remuneration is generally taxed under section 5 of the Income Tax Act (the act), which includes all of the taxpayer's income for a taxation year from an office or employment, including "salary, wages and other remuneration."

Section 6(1)(a) of the act deals with employee benefits and specifies that there shall be included in computing the income of a taxpayer for a taxation year "the value of board, lodging and other benefits of any kind," subject to certain exceptions.

The exceptions listed in section 6(1)(a) include contributions to registered pension funds, private health service plans, group term life and group sickness or accident insurance. These exceptions have been in place since 1948. Section 6 also goes on to deal with certain taxable benefits payable to employees under employee benefit plans or employee trusts.

The benefits exempted from taxation under section 6(1)(a) represent some of the few tax exemptions accorded to ordinary working people. Parliament, for policy reasons, has determined that it is in the public interest to encourage employers to provide certain benefits to employees. This has created a private-sector pension and supplementary benefit system that provides benefits to persons who ordinarily might not be able to afford the actual cost of, for example, supplementary health or dental care, and provides greater retirement income security.

Multiemployer benefit trust funds have arisen as a mechanism for delivering benefits that are tax exempt under section 6(1)(a).

The trust mechanism has also been used to provide taxable benefits, such as vacation pay and prepaid legal service plans. It must be remembered that these trust funds are created essentially to assist bargaining unit employees under collective agreements and are not a common method of executive compensation. The trust acts as a conduit whereby employer contributions are paid to a third-party trustee, who then delivers the benefits to the employees. Accordingly, the trust mechanism is simply an efficient administrative arrangement that permits the delivery of benefits to large groups of employees covered under numerous collective agreements with different employers.

As a matter of tax policy, trusts established to provide employee benefits have not been viewed as a source of tax revenue by Revenue Canada. Certain types of trust funds that provide part of an employee benefit package—such as registered pension plans, group registered retirement savings plans (RRSPs), registered supplementary unemployment benefit plans and certain qualifying vacation pay trust funds—are exempt from taxation on their income pursuant to section 149 of the act.

This is consistent with the policy position that an employee benefit trust fund is not the type of taxpayer that has traditionally provided revenue to the public coffers. Any investment income is usually used for providing the benefits or paying for the administration costs of the fund. The 1979 introduction of the concepts of the employee benefit plan and the employee trust into the act was intended to deal with tax avoidance mechanisms whereby tax deferrals or expanded pension benefits could be obtained, primarily for "executive employees." However, these concepts are applicable in respect of any plans developed to deliver new benefits that are not otherwise tax exempt (e.g., prepaid legal service plans).

The introduction of these provisions in 1979, and the subsequent introduction in 1986 of the retirement compensation arrangement, demonstrated a trend in tax policy to limit the scope of tax-free employee benefits to those currently in existence and to tax any new benefits. The rationale provided for this policy was the equitable tax treatment of all employees, which required that no tax preferences be given to those who were fortunate enough to obtain certain fringe benefits from their employers. The employee benefit plan provisions also ensure that employers deduct their contributions in the same year as the benefits are taxed in the hands of the employee, so that the trust vehicle is not used as a means of deferring taxes.

This expansion of the tax base into the field of employment benefits has occurred at different levels. Provincially, in April 1985, Quebec started a trend when it assessed retail sales tax (RST) on group insurance premiums; Quebec further broadened the tax base in 1990 by extending RST to self-insured benefit arrangements, regardless of the funded status of the benefit plan. Administratively, a pay-as-you-go plan attracted RST at the time of benefit payment, whereas a funded plan was subject to RST at the time of the contribution into the plan.

Then, in its 1993 budget, Quebec effected the most dramatic change to the taxation of benefit plans to date, introducing RST on employer contributions to private health insurance plans (defined as including plans covering medical, hospitalization and dental expenses). It also eliminated the employer's tax exemption for the first $25,000 of group life insurance, subjecting all employer contributions to RST. This eliminated any tax preferential treatment for group term life insurance in Quebec.

In 1993, the Ontario government followed the Quebec model. It extended its RST to insured and self-insured benefits plans, applied equally to funded and unfunded plans. Notably, however, Ontario continues to exempt all contributions to individual life and health plan premiums from RST.

Also in 1993, Ontario expanded its insurance premium tax, a tax on the insurer calculated on the basis of the amount of premiums. Traditionally applied only to insured plans, the premium tax was extended to cover self-insured arrangements.

In 1994, the federal government introduced amendments eliminating the $25,000 income tax exemption on group term life insurance, mirroring the Quebec approach. However, group private health and dental benefits remained exempt from income taxation.

There has clearly been a shift in the taxation of employee benefits. The need for additional revenue to reduce federal and provincial deficits has induced governments to remove the tax sheltering that has historically been provided to traditional employee benefit plans.

UNDERSTANDING THE PROCESS

Why Is It So Hard to Get a Quote?

As can be expected, the first few minutes of any new meeting with a business owner revolve around the "necessity" for a quotation on the benefit plan.

Beep, beep—let's back it up a bit here. Quoting is not always necessary. In fact, a marketing or quoting should only be done once an analysis of current coverage is completed. However, in the event that a measure of the market is necessary, it is always best to understand the process.

Not every business is the same. Each company is as unique as a thumbprint. Different employee bases, distinctive industries, sales cycles, revenue streams, gender splits and target customers all make businesses unique. For all of these reasons and many more, many questions are asked at the onset, and a rate can't just be applied at random.

Consider an individual calling for auto insurance and telling the representative he or she owns a car and needs a rate. Of course, the auto insurer will need to know the make, model, year and condition. So too do group underwriters require the necessary information to provide pricing on benefit plans.

A group benefit plan is unlike most insurance in the marketplace, as it is not just one benefit, such as life insurance or disability coverage; it is several benefits grouped together for the benefit of a group of employees under the same corporate body. Therefore, information must be obtained on the corporation and about the employees to provide accurate pricing.

Customization is key. There's no in-the-box fit for any client. Customers may become benefit partners for several reasons, but they stay because of the customization of the package. Being able to pick and choose what works under their corporate structure is what will also set them apart within their industry when attracting and retaining those valuable resources—employees.

The first step in obtaining pricing on a benefit plan is to ascertain type of company. For instance, are they employing seasonal staff, contract workers or foreign workers, and are they a trucking outfit, machine shop or beauty salon?

Next, what type of plan are they interested in?

- Do they have a plan in place already?
- If so, what kind of plan is it?
- What do they like about this plan?
- What don't they like?
- Why are they seeking alternative advice?
- A plan cannot be improved unless someone takes the time to understand what is going on that has created the conversation.

If clients have no existing coverage in place, then we will want to know what prompted them to look for coverage. What is important to them as employers, and what do they deem important to their employees? What type of coverage are the employees asking for?

By gathering this information and educating the customer, we can be sure to build a plan that will suit their needs and be compatible with their overall business strategy. As mentioned previously, a benefit plan should mirror the compensation strategy and business philosophy of the corporation.

Then there is the most important data—the employee census information: age, gender, occupation, marital status, income and hire date. This information will allow the insurance underwriters to properly price the plan according to the actual data.

Although no one likes to complete paperwork and the questionnaire may, at first glance, seem daunting, remember, the more information provided, the better the proposal. The more accurate the information, the better the ability to build a plan that works for the long term.

TIME FOR A MARKETING

Is a Move Necessary?

Say no to marketing.

When we have the opportunity to meet with a new client, it is typically because they have just received their benefit plan renewal and the rates are increasing. At that time, the expectation from the client is to "market" the benefit plan to seek alternative rates elsewhere.

While many will succumb to that approach, we question what is to be gained without analyzing the plan in detail. It is better to work within the existing provider's parameters and examine all aspects of it. More times than not, an in-depth look at the plan design, claims usage, classification of employees and provider options gives the client the information necessary to make an informed decision. Only then should a market evaluation be performed. Otherwise, clients run the risk wasting their time, which equates to money, with no meaningful results. More times than not, we will continue to work with that client but with the existing insurer.

Prior to considering a change to a new provider, please consider the following.

Are the plans being offered comparable? There are the hidden clauses that are often overlooked when there is the sparkle of savings to be had—least cost alternative drug pricing, prescription formulary restrictions and limited disability, to name but a few. How about technology, ease of administration and claiming options?

Do lower rates mean reduced costs? Are the new rates sustainable given the past usage on the benefit plan? Over time, there is little difference in the rates from one carrier to another based on the same experience information. When all else is equal—number of participants, plan design options and industry—the only change is the amount of benefit usage. This shouldn't be a surprise, as insurers adhere to common actuarial tables and have been quite efficient in reducing claims-processing costs to the lowest possible levels. Based on this, switching on price alone is at best a short-term win that reduces costs below that required to support claims. The result is a tough first and second renewal with the new insurer, and by that time, the process of moving starts all over again.

Then there is the loss of the reserve funding. This is the money set aside (out of the premium dollar) in expectation of the client leaving. This is called "incurred but not reported" (IBNR). With each move to a new provider, the new insurer needs to build up a new reserve. This can account for 8 to 10 percent of the extended health and dental premium built within your first and second renewals. Switching providers leaves money on the table, as you're walking away from your investment and having to pay additional money to build up a new investment. This does not make a lot of financial sense.

The cost of a change to a new carrier can be broken down into two items. The first is the check written to pay the premium. The second is the internal check for time spent by employees (during work time) to manage the benefit plan. This can come by way of administration and by employees reprocessing enrollment forms for switching to another carrier. Often there are better uses of time for all employees than the time it takes to switch insurers.

Each new change creates confusion and can erode employee trust in the employer. It's much like someone deciding for you to change your bank account without asking. As with anything, communication is essential. A common negative message from employees in the midst of changing insurers is that the company must be financially struggling if they are changing carriers to save money. This is especially the case if the plan designs are otherwise the same and the only thing that is changing is the insurer.

Consider your time. The whole exercise can be frustrating and often prove futile. If insanity is defined as "doing the same thing over and over again expecting different results," then marketing without a proper evaluation and analysis is putting you and your staff members on this grinding wheel. Without clear objectives, you could be parting with time and money better spent on improving the business goals.

THE QUOTATION PROCESS

What to Know When Looking for Group Insurance Quotes

One of the first things potential clients typically say at the beginning of the process is, "Insurance is so complicated. There are too many rules." Clients just want what they want and to offer options as they please.

This typically comes on the heel of the fact that the client has to choose one broker to work with in order to receive various insurance quotations from different insurance companies and they have inadvertently called at least two separate insurance brokers figuring that they are the insurance company. In the group benefit world, an insurance carrier (Manulife, Sun Life, Great-West Life, Standard Life, RBC Insurance, etc.) will release only one quote to one broker. In order for another broker to receive a quote on the same client, the original broker must, in essence, be fired from the case.

You see, an insurance broker is not bound by any one insurance company. Brokers are their own companies, and they work for the client—always. An insurance agent, on the other hand, is bound to one insurance company and works for that company only. A client may deal with an agent of that company, but that agent will always be biased toward the insurance company that pays him or her. An example of this is Blue Cross. Brokers can place business with Blue Cross for their clients, but Blue Cross is one of the only remaining insurance companies in Canada who still have their own in-house agents, and when clients calls into Blue Cross for a quotation, they are assigned an agent. Once that agent is assigned, all brokers for that business are blocked.

As a benefit brokers, when a client comes through our doors, going to the marketplace to gather quotations is not the first item on the list, most especially if that client already has a benefit plan in place. The first item is to listen to the wants and needs of that group, recognizing each client is as unique as a fingerprint.

The second item is to complete an analysis of the existing benefit plan to get a real feel for what is going with that benefit plan, which has caused the client to come our way. There is a reason we are at the table instead of the existing broker who placed the business.

The third will be to develop and build a trust of open dialogue and then a plan design, like a blueprint, that is going to work and be able to be modified for that client as they grow and change as a business.

Then and only then will we canvass the marketplace for pricing on benefits, and by that point, all are clear about the objectives of what they want to achieve with the benefit plan as an overall business solution.

Insurance can be complicated by those who like to be complicated, but it doesn't have to be. We like simple, straightforward solutions that work for our clients in attaining their benefit goals.

RETURN ON INVESTMENT

The ROI Necessity

In these tough economic times, ROI (return on investment) is not only a current buzzword but a necessity, not just in business but in our own personal lives as well. ROI is getting the most out of your money. It is your money, after all, and you want it (need it) to last.

When analyzing the following example, it is easy to look at this from a business point of view, but it is necessary to look at it from a personal position as well.

This client owns and operates a business and requires dental work in the amount of $3,588. The client has several options for coverage available, but the primary focus as a consumer is not paying out of pocket for the service. The dentist referred the client to Medicard, a patient finance company or a credit card specifically for health-care services.

With everything set up, the dental services are rendered, and Medicard takes care of the $3,588 bill, treating it as a loan in the client's personal name, not corporate name, repayable over 60 months, with the client paying $105.17 per month.

For that Medicard charges the following:

- 21.95 percent annual interest, which amounts to $2,719.48 over the life of the loan (At this point, many will point out that this client does not have to continue the loan for 60 months; he or she can repay it at any time. True, but anyone following the financial skills of the average Canadian knows without my saying so that most will not repay early. They simply cannot afford to.)
- As well as the one-time grantor's loan finance charge of $215.28

By the time this $3,588 dental bill is repaid, five years after the service, the client would be out of pocket $6,522.76—almost double the original bill! It's like continuing to pay for a sofa that has long since gone out of style and you sold it in a garage sale.

There is, of course, another, better way—a private health services plan (PHSP) for sole incorporated business owners.

Now let's consider the same dental bill of $3,588, only this time the client funds his or her PHSP account (set up in the company name) with corporate money with no sign-up fees. Health and dental services rendered in Canada (outside the province of Quebec) are considered non-taxable, so the corporation does not have to worry about tax consequences of paying for this on behalf of the owner (also considered an employee).

The claim is incurred and there is:

- a 12 percent administration fee charged on the dental bill, amounting to $430.56.
- GST charged on the administration fee, $21.53.

The grand total of the claim treated in this fashion is $4,040.09, creating a savings of $2,473.67 over the Medicard!

Savings is savings, no matter how you slice it, but let's take it just one step further. The $2,473 is not only personal savings for this client, but because the PHSP is in the company name, the full amount of the dental bill becomes a 100 percent corporate tax deduction instead of the client having to repay the Medicard loan personally with after tax dollars, where in order to pay the $105 each month, the client had to earn $143!

Therein lies significant ROI.

COST SHARING

Options for Splitting the Costs

The means of funding the benefit program should be done in the most effective and efficient manner. There are a number of areas you should review in terms of tax implications, employee participation and management of expenses.

Tax Implications

The chart on the following page illustrates the favorable tax treatment available to corporations versus individuals with respect to premiums. We have demonstrated the impact of funding on the payment of a benefit through the plan.

Having employees use after-tax dollars to fund premiums is a much more expensive route to follow when a company is able to utilize pre-tax income to pay for benefits. The only employee-paid premiums that deliver any tax benefit are long-term disability and life insurance. Other than these areas, it is clearly more efficient to have the company fund the plan.

Employee Participation

Changes to the cost-sharing arrangement may favorably impact the employee's participation in your plan. Appropriate participation means adequate sharing of risk, which will lead to a more manageable plan for the future. The risk of anti-selection is minimized as well.

Managed Control

Today, employers are expected to provide health and dental plans, which are rising in cost (according to some estimates) at a rate of 10 percent to 15 percent per year. For most companies, this is simply not supportable long term. Employers are now looking to their advisers to provide creative solutions to manage these costs.

An employee-funded program results in an employee-controlled program. Economic reality requires some difficult decisions. The time-consuming and personalized involvement of employees will make appropriate management of the plan virtually impossible.

To ensure continued delivery of a fair and comprehensive benefits program, corporate management is critical.

RATE INCREASES

The First Renewal after the Switch

The definition of insanity is doing the same thing over and over again and expecting a different result.

When companies switch their insurance provider due to a rate hike at their renewal with a previous carrier, in many cases, without understanding why the premiums increased to begin with, business owners have simply "bought" themselves a one-year reprieve before the new carrier increases their rates for the same reasons as the previous, and these increases can often be more substantial than what would have been incurred over the two years with the incumbent carrier.

In these scenarios, the question amounts to "Why did you move in the first place?"

No matter what, there is no way to get around the simple equation: usage, plus administration, plus inflation, equals the premium. All insurance providers are a business first and operate in this environment.

Though we all want something for nothing, that is not the case—ever. An insurance carrier is no different from any other business. When it comes to claims, they need to have the funds available to cover the usage, especially on the day-to-day choice benefits, including dental, vision care and paramedical services, such as massage therapy. This prior usage is a significant factor for creating new rates.

But if you have moved without understanding the essence of the benefit package, you could be setting yourself up to pay more over the long term. The following is some industry information, which may impact your decision to move or continue to work with the existing provider.

- Most group underwriter expenses are within percentage points of one another. When a marketing has been conducted on your behalf, beware of those carriers who promise substantial savings based on the same information as the other carriers. This may be an indicator that they are "buying" the business in anticipation that you will not move again so quickly at the first renewal.
- True rates from the providers are what the industry refers to as the "manual" rates, and these are typically within 10 percent of each other based on a company's demographics and industry code. In order to be competitive, insurers may discount these manual rates, but again, once the business is secured, they recoup this discount at the first renewal.
- Each time a business moves to a new insurance benefit provider, they have to reestablish reserves. These reserves are referred to as "incurred but not reported" (IBNR). This reserve can account for 8 to 10 percent of the rate. With every move, this reserve fund is left behind with the old carriers and has to be reestablished within the first year with the new provider. This does not form part of the initial quotation on which you based your decision to move in the first place.
- Inflation charges for health and dental range from 11 to 15 percent depending on the benefit line and are factored at the first renewal. When quoting, the insurance carrier does not typically factor these numbers into the rates. They are applied at the first renewal.
- The unforeseen consequence of a move typically include the timing of the move. For instance, many maximums are set at a calendar year, but if you changed carriers in August, by all accounts, employees could use a full year of maximum eligibility within those first four months, and then the maximum is reset January 1, and they can reuse again. So the first renewal may be

impacted by two years' worth of maximum usage, and the new carrier will want their money.
- Let's not forget the hidden costs of a move—the time spent organizing the paperwork; coordinating employees to complete new forms; establishing the online presence; and dealing with banking information, new booklets, education meetings and employee anxiety relative to the change, which may impact their trust in the value of the benefits being offered.

The bottom line is this: no matter what, employers need to be aware of their plan design and usage patterns. Unless these items are addressed, they have simply placed themselves on the hamster wheel to repeat the same pattern over and over again without changing the result.

DRIVERS OF HEALTH CARE COSTS

Increasing Exponentially

It is no secret the cost of health care is on a steady, if not exponential, increase in Canada—and globally for that matter.

Canadian health-care cost drivers include the following:

- demographics, population growth and aging
- price inflation
- technology
- utilization

As we have focused on the technology and utilization previously, this will concentrate on the first two: demographics and price.

Health care costs now exceed, for the most part, the rate of economic growth. Prescription drugs continue to grow at a rate of more than 10 percent to 15 percent per year. In the next decade, as the baby boomers enter their mid-to-late seventies—the age when usage of the health-care system begins to rise dramatically—we can expect even more burden placed on this floundering system.

The "Health Care Cost Drivers: The Facts" report released from the Canadian Institute for Health Information illustrates how Canada spends more on health care than the average for Organization for Economic Co-operation and Development member countries, but not by much. Average annual health spending in the 34 industrialized countries was $3,590 per capita in 2012, or 9.4 percent of gross domestic product.

"Physician spending has been amongst the fastest-growing health category in recent years, increasing at an annual rate of 6.8 percent per year from 1998 to 2008. More than one–half of this growth, 3.6 percent per year, is attributed to increases in physician fee schedules."

Much of the focus on the health-care needs of Canada's aging population surrounds the shortage of physicians with expertise in geriatric care. But the country's seventy-five thousand licensed physicians represent only a small part of the Canadian health-care workforce. By contrast, there are approximately three hundred sixty thousand regulated nurses, thirty-five thousand social workers, thirty thousand pharmacists, seventeen thousand physiotherapists, thirteen thousand occupational therapists and ten thousand dietitians in Canada.

Improving care for Canadian older adults will undoubtedly require educating and engaging the entire health-care workforce.

Offering or finding benefit solutions for this segment of the population continues to be a hot topic.

- To what age can seniors continue to have coverage under the group benefit plan when they are actively at work?
- What benefits are seniors entitled to?
- What are the retirement options for these valued employees?
- How can boomers plan for the additional costs into their golden years?

These are great questions with excellent answers. Find out more.

BENEFIT PRICING

Moving Carriers on Price Alone

MP Benefits Inc. is a business in business for businesses, and as such, our thermometer always reflects the mood of the economy. When our clients hurt, we hurt.

In the last year, with the combination of a downward economy, the increase to minimum wage and additional taxes on the horizon, never mind the increased marginal tax rate and job loss, business is tough all over. Retaining a benefit plan in this environment is hard enough, but add to this toxic mix a tough renewal that proposes to increase rates.

Just as there are a number of factors adding to the tough times in Alberta, there are several realities impacting the cost structure of the benefit plan:

- an aging population
- increased disability claims
- employees pending layoff using the benefit plan the maximum
- retained employees using as much of the benefit plan as an entitlement in the event it suddenly be cancelled
- fewer participants left holding the bag of increased costs (to pay the bill)

Before running off to conduct a market study to shop for better rates, as in anything else related to business, take a moment to analyze and find out exactly what is going on with the benefit plan. After close to two decades as benefit specialists, we can see that groups who have moved carriers several times over the years to achieve better rates are no further ahead than those who have remained consistently with the existing carrier. In fact, I would suggest those who have retained their benefit plan with the existing carrier, capitalizing on longevity, broader policy wording, among other factors, are in fact better off price-wise.

Attack the Problem Strategically

Plan Design

As the benefit plan should mirror both the overall business plan and the compensation strategy for the employees, like both of those items, the plan design does need to be tweaked from time to time to remain consistent. Trim the fat, retain the necessary insurance items and perhaps look at better options to provide enhancements while staying within the allotted budget. A good example would be the core benefits, removing the paramedical services, vision care and major restorative and orthodontic dental and opting to add in a health spending account to take care of these additional benefit options but within a set limit. Instead of being seen as a takeaway, employees appreciate the flexibility and control of using their benefit dollars where they need them most.

Rates

Without question, demographic changes impact the insurance costs. Remember, group is essentially one-year term insurance, and we age. When the renewal comes around, even if the plan members have remained consistent, they are still one year older. Given the aging workforce and the amount of disability claims on the insured books, most employers can expect a 5 to 8 percent increase for life and disability rates, depending on the male-to-female split and the change in covered numbers from one year to the next.

Understand the numbers: pharmacy, professional services (massage, chiro, physio, etc.), health services, vision and dental care services are priced based upon usage (claims), plus the administration expenses to process the claims, adjusted for inflation, looking a trending measures year over year, to arrive at the projected premium expectation. Just as you are in business to make money, cover expenses and make ends meet, so too is the insurer or benefits provider.

There are always cheaper plans—but you get what you pay for. Don't sacrifice critical coverage for paying for the same service with after-tax dollars. If we can all agree that the number-one reason to have a benefit plan in the first place is the tax advantage, we must ensure the rates match the coverage, which will then protect the dollars spent, keeping them in a tax-friendly environment.

The best way to handle a tough renewal is to clearly understand if the renewal is accurate or fair. If it is, you now have your new baseline for what you are offering in coverage. Take the time to understand discounting, inflation adjustments, manual rates, funding arrangements and your usage. Then you can decide how to reduce your costs if you are not comfortable with where the correct premium sits.

THE EVER-INCREASING RATES

Paying for Overusage

It's true—everyone wants a benefit plan, and no one wants to pay. It's like having a fender bender and groaning when the renewal comes up. Insurance was great when it took care of the bills, but it's not so great when the rates come due. Remembering that the purpose of insurance is to mitigate loss, the premiums, in most situations, are retroactive after claims, and the increases are spread among the many, so no one company ever bears the full burden of covering the entire cost to recover the claimed amount.

At the risk of a groan and to change the conversation, let's view benefits from the perspective of an investment—an investment into your employees' wellbeing, an investment into the corporate entity and the financial security healthy employees will create.

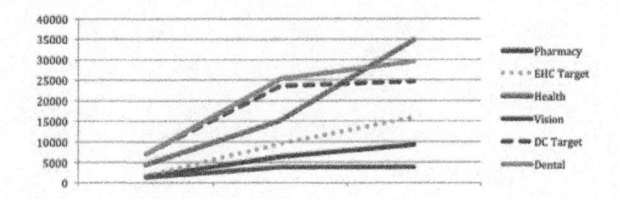

Check out the wedge between health claims used and the expected target for claims. For every dollar paid in premium, $1.69 was returned to the plan members in the form of claims. By any investment scenario, that is an excellent return. Yes, of course the rates were increased, but they were not increased by 70 percent—not even half that!

Education and consultation are key in these situations. The last two years have been brutal for employers. They have undergone massive employee layoffs, whereby the employees have used every penny allowable under the benefit program prior to termination, leaving those left on the plan to pay the costs.

Moving insurance providers is an option, and many have chosen this path. But in the same manner that the current carrier has the 69 percent return on investment, this change in providers will offer only another year's grace before an even larger increase is faced and you stand to lose coverage, never mind more money in making the change.

Hidden cost factors include lack of comparable coverage. Is the plan truly apples to apples? And how much time (equal to money) did it take to make this change—including new enrollment, new administration and new claiming parameters?

A much better approach is to face and address the issue at hand—employee usage, combined with the plan design offering. How can your broker work with you to design a plan that covers off the essentials, while trimming the fat to bring the costs back in line? A good example is if massage therapy is the main culprit of excessive claims, how much will be saved in premium dollars by removing the coverage?

We are proud to turn benefits on its edge, and sometimes that means turning the conversation as well. We're looking forward to our next chat.

TARGET LOSS RATIOS

What Is the Impact of TLRs on Benefit Pricing?

Target Loss Ratio

It is important to understand the concept of a target loss ratio (TLR) when examining the renewal rate basis developed by a carrier. The TLR represents the percentage of every dollar for experience-rated benefits that they expect to pay out in the form of claims. The difference between the TLR and 100 percent represents the carrier operational expense charges for managing the program.

For smaller cases, the TLR is utilized in only part of the rate basis calculation. In smaller groups, the claims experience is not considered credible; that is, your actual results are believed on a small percentage of the time. The larger the case, the higher the overall experience-rated premium, and this generates a higher credibility factor. This approach is consistent throughout the marketplace with all carriers.

To illustrate, if your group had a loss ratio of 50 percent on the extended health and the target loss ratio was 68 percent, you might expect to see the following calculation:

claims × inflation / trend / utilization / target loss ratio
= required premiums - fully credible rate basis
50% × 115% / 68% = 84.6% = -15.4%
Claims × inflation / trend / utilization × credibility factor + carrier manual rates × TLR × inflation / trend / utilization × credibility factor / TLR = required premiums - partially credible rate basis.
50% × 115% × 30% = 17.25
75% × 115% × 70% = 60.38
Total 77.63 / 68 TLR = +14.2% increase

The reason your own results are not fully credible is that the risk of fluctuation in results is far greater on a group with 20 lives than on a group with 100 lives. Risk cannot be spread as easily in smaller cases. This approach affords you some protection in years where results are very poor because a very good experience is only partially credible, so a very poor experience is considered only partially credible.

MISSING THE SHOE BOX

Technology—love it! Can't live without it. But sometimes, I shake my head and wonder if I'm better off without all of these "advancements"—applications, ease of use systems and streamlined access.

Consider, we are only a couple of decades into point-of-sale drug cards and claim submission from the dentist direct to the insurer. Gone are the days of the shoe box and saving up claims for bulk submission for reimbursement. Don't get me wrong, these advancements are all good. Online and smartphone services save the consumer—the employee—time, energy, effort and, a lot of times, frustration. The acceleration of claims processing and reimbursement means a claim submitted digitally today can be in the employee's bank account tomorrow. Wow. That's fast.

But there's a cost to the digital age.

The speed of technological advancement has also created an increased claiming opportunity. There's no missed opportunity—nothing left in the shoe box. There's an attitude of entitlement from plan members that everything should be claimable, while at the same time, the consumer has lost a fundamental appreciation for just how much is spent on benefits—perhaps billions of dollars each year in Canada—because they are not paying out of pocket for it first. The direct claim submission has meant a reduced awareness of the actual costs and amount of claiming activity.

Consider how many times I facilitate an employee meeting where the number-one rebuke to rate hikes is, "I don't use the plan." Yes, they went to the dentist twice that year, as did the spouse and children. A few prescriptions, vision and let's not forget the occasional massage, yet because everything was direct processing, the perception of actual claim activity diminished. What likely amounted to between $3,000 and $4,000 in claims had the perception of a couple hundred dollars because that was all they were out of pocket due to coinsurance. Because there is no little out-of-pocket expense, no one can blame the average employee for this perception. Yet these false perceptions—the lack of awareness of claim activity—devalues the benefit plan overall.

It's true, digital innovations are transforming health care, with huge implications for benefit plan sponsors and the employees they serve. There are estimated to be between 800 and 1,000 health-care-related technology start-ups in Canada today.

The big question is, how do employers create an awareness of the plan's value, while maintaining the ease to which employees have come to appreciate their claims being reimbursed?

We are always open to suggestions.

IF IT'S NOT BROKEN—WHY FIX IT?

Remember your first cell phone? Perhaps it was the old brick that looked like a World War II field communication telephone. Perhaps yours was the Motorola flip phone, which sold 130 million units after its global launch in 2004. Whatever version is remembered fondly, those are likely not broken either. Yet like horses used mainly for transport, consumers have moved on.

The problem is never the problem. The problem is not knowing how to think about the problem.

If we can agree that changing the methods of how we communicate—how we transport goods to both improve efficiency, as well offer a better reflection of future growth—does it not stand reason that a benefit plan developed to reflect the corporate philosophy will, at some point, have to upgraded?

This does not necessitate a change in the current provider, simply a better understanding of the design and what other "benefits" may be available for the ever-savvy and diverse workforce.

Remember, at the time, the Razr flip phone was one of the most iconic phones ever designed. Then BlackBerry released the first prominent smartphone of its kind, specializing in secure communications. This moved the phone from simply providing voice communications to a mobile productivity centre in the palm of the hand. It was a leader—until the iPhone.

Now, in the 25 years since Tim Berners-Lee made the World Wide Web available to the public, more than half of the world's population uses a smartphone, spending approximately $800 annually on the phone, applications, music and video combined. It's all to improve daily life.

Sometimes, though, when it comes to benefits, if you've seen one, you've seen them all. There is next to no difference between one and another. Has the cost of consumable goods not increased? Has the evolution of technology not broken through to include health services? Of course they have. However, benefit plans continue down the archaic path of redundancy. Employers are unwilling to change a plan that "is not broken," thinking this may mean a change in carrier, more work and equivalent hassles better avoided.

That is not so.

By not exploring the evolution of the benefit plan, employers leave themselves open to offering a program that no longer addresses the reality of their changing and diverse workforce. As a compensation strategy, benefits can be a tool to recruit and retain employees.

Consider what it would mean to overall productivity to implement a plan with increased flexibility and more choice, understanding that compensation by today's standards isn't just pay. It includes salary, pension, benefits and all investments, including training to represent the total rewards of employment.

Tragically, though, only about 30 percent of companies today offer truly flexible plans.

Strategically, an employer's greatest competitive advantage is its people, because productivity and innovation come from employees. Investing in these valuable assets means providing wellness programs focused to optimize work-life balance and encourage healthier lifestyles.

Numerous studies over the years have concluded comprehensive wellness programs have a significant return on investment for employers. A 2010 Harvard University meta-analysis of the literature on costs and savings associated with wellness programs found the return-on-investment on medical costs was $3.27 for every dollar spent.

In conclusion, though the benefit plan may not be broken, that doesn't mean it doesn't need fixing.

COMMODITY

Are group benefits a commodity or an investment?

Put another way, are they expendable? Are benefits at the tail end of the business plan? Are they only placed when or if there is enough disposable income to warrant the expense?

If that is the case, then it's no wonder there are so many cookie cutter, set and leave it plans that are not valued or appreciated by the employees in which they are supposed to be benefiting.

An employee group benefit program should be implemented with thought and precision. A well-designed plan should always and forevermore mirror the corporate philosophy, be a party to the business plan and form the foundation of the compensation strategy. And for those reasons, it should be seen as an investment, not an expendable commodity.

No matter how small the organization, every business that considers the implementation of an employee group benefit program deserves value for the dollars spent. Value comes from creating a blueprint of what is necessary—deciding ultimately what the corporation wants to achieve through the implementation.

Customization removes commoditization for employee group benefits. When benefits are placed that lack a custom-designed plan, then entitlement is encouraged, and the perception turns to seeing the employee group benefits as expendable.

Today's benefit plans feature innovative products developed with the end user in mind. Streamlined efficiencies allow for often same-day claim processing, instantaneous point-of sale electronic processing, Visa platform solutions and smartphone applications with photo-processing technology.

Benefits are not all about health and dental claims. Today's plans take into account the need for work-life balance. Workplace wellness, disability management, wage replacement, employee assistance, critical illness and mental stability are now foundation markers for a solidly built program.

Like a well-built car, when you get what you want, rest assured it will get you where you need to go—safely and without incident. Price will follow. The same is true in employee group benefits. Taking the time to properly build a program designed specifically for the corporate workforce and the unique needs of your industry, purposely working within the fundamental guidelines of what makes your business a success, will ensure the price point always matches and falls in line with budget expectations.

Partnering with a broker who understands the blueprint approach to benefits will build an innovative, comprehensive program, valued by the workforce over the long term, because it supports employees when they need it—as they need it.

DISCOUNTS

Current pricing practices in group insurance markets are creating something of a feeding frenzy among insurance carriers looking to maintain existing accounts or win new ones. For some time, market-discount practices have become the norm where insured rates look more attractive than they might have been in the past.

Two questions come to mind:

1. First, how long can the practice last?
2. Are these accepted rates in the client's best interest?

The answers are somewhat vague: "Who knows?" and "Maybe."

Then how are these discounts made possible?

There are a couple of principal sources for these marketing discounts. The profitability of life and disability policies may be subsidizing health and dental insured rates at or even below claims. Also, carriers may be blessed by having additional cash resources on their books that may be channeled into providing market discounts to acquire new business, which may be recaptured on renewal should the groups exhibit poor claims experience or spread across other group clients.

The group business is pretty simple. Carriers collect premiums and pay for claims, leaving enough back from the collected premium to pay expenses (adjudication, administration, risk, commissions, premium tax, etc.) and an acceptable profit. The long-term viability of the plan is predicated on the way the carrier manages the cost of claims.

Today's claims are tomorrow's premiums.

Short-term price fluctuations make it possible for a carrier to buy business, but at some point, the piper has to be paid, and years of unprofitability will have to be made good with rate increases to return the carrier's profit and loss statement from red ink to black.

Why is this happening?

An opinion: most of the carriers in the Canadian market are either publicly traded or have major shareholder groups. Bay Street considers top-line revenue, revenue growth and utilization of cash resources as key indicators of financial strength, understanding that company profitability may be a key metric somewhat in flux from year to year. A certain amount of deal flow is vital to keep carrier cash flow circulating and in use, which may manifest itself in the market as market discounts or allowances.

Plan sponsors, the employers, need to recognize that no two carriers pay claims the same way. It's incumbent on consumers and their advisers alike to make sure their chosen carrier is among the best in controlling costs.

Accepted cost control methods of cutting benefits, raising co-insurance levels or raising rates are poor substitutes for sound plan management and won't serve anyone well when premiums return to a state of normalcy.

Carriers can maintain discounted premiums only so long before they need to raise rates. When that happens, sponsors will either have to pay up or shop around to move the plan again.

The high cost of moving the plan in real terms and lost productivity must be factored into the equation. The amount of disruption to members and internal administration staff alike must also be considered.

Plan sponsors must learn to choose between the stability of working a sustainable plan provided by carriers who pay attention to claims management and resist the lure of upfront marketing discounts and the continual upheaval of shopping and hopping. The result is that plan sponsors may begin to feel disillusioned, lured in with great rates only to find that the next guy gets an even better deal at their expense when they see their first post-guarantee-period renewal.

At some point, quick-turn groups may find it difficult to find carriers willing to quote.

Reprinted with permission from, Kelly Jardine, account executive, SunAdvantage Edmonton Group Office.

MORE THAN DOLLARS

Money Is Not the Motivator

Wealth matters—don't get me wrong. But with the newest generation coming into the workforce, cash is no longer the motivator it once was.

Sure, money's exciting and tempting, and people have been seen to do almost anything for it—in the short term. How about the long haul?

Assuming you are not hiring employees on a contractual, short-term basis, then providing a long-term approach would be valuable.

In his book *Drive: The Surprising Truth about What Motivates Us*, Daniel Pink debates the "If, then" issue of money: "If you do this job for me, then I will pay you X dollars. If you continue to do this, better, faster and consistently, then I will pay you more."

With more than 40 years of research behind his studies, he found that because of the technology and the move toward a work-life attitude, money over the long term will not motivate the work force. In his words, "You can no longer entice someone with a sweeter carrot or threaten them with a sharper stick."

As employers, we need to cater to the perceived lifestyle experience. These right-brained employees need to feel they are part of the company. Millennials are creative, conceptual thinkers, driving and making the business move forward faster and more productively than it ever had in the past. These employees require different compensation to keep them motivated. They need the following:

- Autonomy: the urge for control, to direct their own lives and their lives within the company as it surrounds them
- Mastery: the desire to get better and better at what they do, to own their position and have a sense of mastery
- Purpose: being involved strategically in something larger then themselves

Yes, money is important and should be established at the onset. From that point on, motivation through lifestyle will impact an employee over the long term. Protection for them and their family members when it matters most and the promise of the continuation of their existing lifestyle in the event something catastrophic should happen will ultimately create that long-term motivator to retain key employees.

THE PAIN OF CHANGE VERSUS THE COST OF SAME

> Change happens when the pain of staying the same is greater than the pain of change.
>
> —Tony Robbins

It comes down to dollars and sense, really.

Many times employers view their benefit plan as an expense—a commodity—a perk, disposable. A company's greatest resource is the employees who assist in growth and revenue generation, creating success in their chosen marketplace. Retention of these assets is a necessity, and benefit plans are often the number-one factor, far outweighing salary, in determining whether to stay or go.

When it comes time to review the benefit plan, though, choices sometimes seem limited. You can change insurance carriers or suffer through the renewal for yet another year.

Adjust your perspective. Have a conversation.

Staying the same is costing money. Contrary to the common conception, changing doesn't have to involve switching insurance providers. What about contacting a specialist who can find a solution? Delve into the nitty gritty of what the benefits offer and compensation strategy it is supposed to enhance. Finding a solution will save money.

Change is simple, but it isn't easy. It's not complicated, but it's hard.

By paying attention to what matters to the employer, a specialist can design a benefit program to mesh with both the financial and compensation packages. In the marketplace, it staggering to see how many benefit plans increase in cost year after year, yet offer no new functionality, no alternative options, nothing to encourage employers to see it as anything other than an ever-increasing cost. It's time to change the perspective from expense to an investment.

Relationships matter.

We understand companies are prepared to continue to invest in solutions only if the price is right. By creating a partnership with the specialist, both parties will work to a common successful end.

BUYER BEWARE

Price Isn't Everything

It happens in every business; clients are lost.

Clients can be lost for any number of reasons—poor service, better opportunity elsewhere, change of decision maker—but very often it all comes down to cost.

What is lost, though, when it is all about price?

As a business in business for businesses, every time a client is lost, it is not just a loss to us as the broker but a loss to all we partner with to ensure the best of the best for that client. The loss of one client impacts many.

From our perspective, we gained a client into the fold many years ago at a time when their when their business was in a flux, let's say. They were downsizing and sadly the type of business that is quickly becoming an endangered species. (Much like a horseshoe company when people began using motorized vehicles.) Working to restructure their plan, retaining them with existing providers, we managed to trim fat and retain the valuable bits that were important to employees. We analyzed needs versus wants. When there was a problem getting the bills paid, we went to bat for the client, buying them time. It's these types of extras and more that we do because each client is different and so there is no hard and fast mold. Remember, we treat every client as though they were our only client. We don't say, "No, that's above and beyond." We listen and strive to understand their point of view, and if we or someone in our trusted circle can assist, we simply do.

Now the company is stable and moving forward.

One would think over time, a good working relationship develops based on goodwill, loyalty and a developed, trusted relationship. Then, out of the blue, the client says, "We've decided to go elsewhere."

Whoa, where did that come from? What happened? Where did we let you down? Why weren't we included in the tender process?

The answer is "No, it is nothing you did. Service was fine. We just decided it was time for a change."

It happens, yes. People keep telling me, "Don't take it personally." But you know what? This is a personal business, a relationship business, and if I didn't take it personally, I really shouldn't be in this business.

Others ask, "Would you do it again?" The simple answer is yes. The longer answer is "Yes, we actually continue to do that sort of thing every day!"

Going above and beyond keeps us striving for our clients. Doing what we do because we simply love what we do and being able to provide the extras is what it is all about.

I'm proud to say many who opt for change due to price often return to the fold, and we gladly welcome them back.

GETTING THE CLAIM PAID

Knowing What Is and Is Not Covered and Why

Coping with the news that you or a loved one is ill can be stressful, and deciding upon the proper treatments is your top priority. But what happens if your claim is declined?

You can challenge the decision—and even succeed in reversing it. The Patient Advocate Foundation advises taking the following steps to successful claims payment.

1. Get it in writing.

The denial should state specific reasons why your claim was refused. You'll need to counter these arguments in an appeal letter.

2. Request a copy of your insurance booklet.

Read and understand the language of your plan, especially sections that deal with treatments and appeals of denied claims. If something doesn't make sense, ask for assistance.

3. Know the illness and the treatment plan.

You will be better prepared to work with the insurance company if you understand your diagnosis. Discuss issues with your doctor until you fully comprehend your condition and why the procedure in question is necessary.

4. Gather documents.

Letters from your doctor that explain your diagnosis and treatment, including success rate, are essential. Any articles about procedures in medical journals and copies of relevant documents from your own medical records are also helpful.

5. Write the first appeals letter.

Be sure to include your policy number as well as your identification number. Explain why you think the decision to deny your treatment was wrong. Keep a copy of everything you submit.

6. Be patient.

Keep a journal to record any contact with the insurer, including the names and phone numbers of the people you speak to as well as what was discussed. No matter what the response to your appeal—approval or a second denial—get it in writing. If your claim is denied again, don't give up. Read the reasons carefully; they could be different.

7. Keep accurate records.

A no from the insurance company on your claim does not have to be the final word. Just remember these six steps:

- Get it in writing.
- Be informed on your coverage. Have the benefit booklet handy.
- Know the illness and the chosen treatment and why that treatment is the right choice.
- Gather documentation.
- Be in charge. Write your own appeal letter.

And always be patient. This cycle may take a couple of times to be successful.

Remember, never give up. In some cases, three or four appeals may be necessary.

HSA ADMINISTRATION FEES

What Are You Getting for the Fees Paid?

Are you getting the most out of the health spending account for the fees you pay?

Every discussion, as it should, comes back to the most effective use of your dollar

Health spending accounts offer 100 percent tax-free benefits to employees and 100 percent corporate tax deductions for the employer.

But for the money spent on administration, you are getting smartphone applications, real-time processing, and online claims administration. The market is incredibly competitive right now. Don't fall for administration savings for six months or a year. Benefit providers will lock in your low administration for the life of the contract.

Find the best provider for you.

Section 3

Plan Design
Building Compensation

PLAN DESIGN MATTERS

The Foundation

Just as a house requires a blueprint prior to construction, an objective to provide a solid foundation, so too does a company require a stable and effective plan design to offer benefits that work.

Many programs sold on price die on price. They haven't paid attention to the blueprint. Perhaps an outline was never established. Over time, cracks appear in the foundation to highlight situations and a multitude of problems. At that time, the employer begins to question why the company is paying for something that does not cover the needs or the wants of the employees and why no one knew about exclusions and limitations on coverage. It's not like it is fine print. It is simply the plan never formed part of the conversation. Everything was knee-jerk in favour of concentrating on costs.

Generalists will often overlook that a properly designed, well-thought-through strategy, developed for the unique needs of that employer group will cost less over the long term than a plan riddled with exclusions and limitations on coverage in order to keep the costs low for the first year.

Areas often overlooked or skimmed include LCA (least cost alternative) for drug claims, which should not be confused with a generic equivalent drug definition. Least cost means just that—the least-costing drug within that drug family.

What about the requirement for a prescription for paramedical professional services, such as massage, chiropractic, etc.? This makes making claims more cumbersome to an employee, who has to make an appointment with his or her general practitioner doctor and wait to get into see that doctor for a simple referral in order to make the claim. What happens if the employee has gone for the services first because he or she "didn't know"? Claims are rejected in full, and the employee walks away unhappy and spreads the unhappy news with coworkers, thereby eroding the fundamental purpose of an employee benefit plan developed for the satisfaction of employees.

Another bone of contention for people making claims is the dental fee guide when the employee attends a dentist who is non-compliant with the averages applied for dental claims. Now the employee is out-of-pocket, with after-tax dollars for these extra charges.

Implementing an "I thought" benefit is common as well—group critical conditions versus group critical illness insurance. Having an "any occupation" disability definition as compared to an "own occupation" is as different as night and day when it comes to making a claim.

Take the time to review the benefit plan design with a professional to ensure the coverage is what you not only want it to be but also what it needs to be when you need it to be there for you and the employee members.

SO I CAN UNDERSTAND THEM

The greatest compliment any salesman can receive is when their clients tell them they explained the product or service in way they could understand it and apply it back to their own business practice.

The insurance arena is polluted with jargon. It's as though many years ago someone thought if they could make the process so complicated, no one would ask questions and instead simply nod their head and purchase. The reality is the less people understand benefits, by the time they are at my door, it takes hip waders to get though all of the misconceptions.

In an era where communication is as abundant as it is available from the Internet and social media sites, you would think it would be easier to understand both insurance and benefits options, but it's not. It's not because of the legalities involved in miscommunication. Saying something or putting something out there can be misconstrued by the reader and ops. "Houston, we have problem." Stakeholders over-talk and continue to complicate things.

Misinformation

Being different is part of what we do, so we'll put all that worry about legalities aside for a moment and hope you will read this in the light it is meant, and we'll try to explain benefits so we can all understand them.

Life insurance is the lottery that always pays out. Employees pay premiums each month (purchase your ticket each week), and eventually someone wins because it's the one sure thing.

When it comes to group benefits, life insurance, accidental death and dismemberment (AD&D), dependent life insurance and long-term disability are four of the most common insured products. Pure insurance includes risk of loss of life and risk of loss of income.

Pricing for these products is not significantly different from one insurance carrier to another as the rating is typically based on the same national information on death and disability actuary tables. So if we consider these four as the insured side of our benefits, then pricing for these benefits would be much like going to the pumps for gas. There really is little difference on price going from PetroCan to Shell to Husky. What makes the difference is the grade of gas (in each consumer's opinion) and the size of the tank (i.e., filling a smart car for ten dollars and filling a Hummer for a hundred dollars). The size of the tank means how much insurance is being purchased.

The other side of the benefit plan is a place where consumers live from day to day; that includes the prescription drugs, health-care services and vision and dental care. We'll refer to these benefits as experience benefits because they are based on consumer usage. Think of these benefits like going to the grocery store—Sobeys, IGA, Safeway, SuperSave, Overweightea, etc. At any one of the big grocery chains, the price difference between the same cut of beef can be significant depending on how much is required, the supply the store has on hand, their supplier for the product and even perhaps the time of the year (barbecue season, for example) it is being purchased.

Shopping for these benefits takes strategy and knowhow. The plan design or list of benefits (groceries) that are necessary for your company makes a big difference in price. Are we shopping for the blue no-name label or Campbell's soup, which is like having prescription drug coverage that defines the prescription reimbursement as that which is prescribed by a doctor (Campbell's soup) or the no-name blue-label version of the least cost alternative drug definition for reimbursement.

Some may say, "Well, what's the difference besides taste and texture? It's soup." Still, choice goes deeper than that. Consumers only really notice if they are the ones eating the soup.

Providing coverage just to say there is a plan in place is one thing. Providing coverage or benefits that actually meet people's expectations is what makes the difference. For the person who requires prescriptions, a least cost alternative makes all the difference and after-tax money out of their pocket, as well as value of the benefits in the eyes of the end user.

Just as an FYI, least cost alternative (LCA) means if the medication prescribed is within an interchangeable grouping of medications (with the same active ingredients, dosage and form), the program may pay only up to the least cost alternative (LCA) price if one has been established for that grouping. As a consumer, I may be prescribed a prescription for cholesterol that has a generic equivalent; however, because there is a least cost alternative for cholesterol, my plan with the LCA attached will only cover the lowest-cost cholesterol drug available, which may not suit my medical needs as intended by my doctor.

Having a good benefit plan doesn't mean busting the pocketbook. It means knowing what you are purchasing the right products for you.

BENEFIT RESOLUTIONS

Planning Matters

The Benefits of a Strategic Resolution

With each passing year, in this current economy, we all know every dollar counts. Planning for sustainability this coming year is a must for the New Year's resolutions list.

As a business owner, you could be leaving a lot of money on the table if you don't take the time to analyze and more importantly, understand the true value of employee benefits.

The number-one reason to have a benefit plan is tax. For three letters, tax imbues such an emotional response in most business owners that it needs to be capitalized. But tax in relation to a benefit plan works favourably for both the employer and the employee. All premiums paid by an employer are a corporate tax deduction. Because the employer is an employee of the corporation, all benefit expenses claimed and paid as a result of health or dental, in the same manner as other employees, are all non-taxable (outside the province of Quebec).

Never underestimate the value of nontaxable benefits. On an average 20-person group, claims can amount to between $30,000 to $40,000 in any given year. This compounds the larger the group. If these employees could not process the expenses through a benefit plan, they would be paying with after-tax money, which could amount to an additional $14,000 a year out of their pocket aside from the claim itself. Running these costs through a benefit plan, that same $14,000 is now savings because it is not applicable, plus the employer claims all of the premium paid as a corporate tax deduction. A win-win scenario!

This is the reason why a benefit plan should mirror the corporate strategy and be assessed and analyzed annually. The true value of the benefit plan should be outlined to employees per their compensation package, as benefits form a significant part of the total rewards of employment.

The following are some considerations for your 2017 benefit plan resolutions.

Understand the benefit summary: Get to know the definitions and exclusions. You may think you have coverage, less the co-insurance, only to find out the expense is limited or excluded due to definitions, fee-guide schedules, formularies, deductibles, etc.

Health spending accounts: Is there a "fit" within your plan options for this form of self-insurance, especially for expenses such as massage, vision, major dental and orthodontics? Setting an overall maximum to be used where the employees need it most is typically more cost effective than paying premiums for defined coverage that may or may not be utilized.

Employee meetings: Offering sound advice and educating employees on claim submission, coordination of benefits, online access, their maximums and whom to contact when they have questions or concerns will relieve the burden from the plan administrator and reinforce the value of the benefit plan.

Financial fitness: Implementing a pension plan, group RRSP or deferred profit sharing plan (DPSP) through the corporation for the employees means lower fees than are typically available through retail, no penalties for switching between investments and professional money management.

Employee assistance programs (EAP): For a small fee, these programs offer great value and keep employees actively engaged, but more importantly, focused on work by allowing them the opportunity to seek professional help for those money problems, marriage breakdown and children with learning disabilities—issues that make it hard to function at work.

Working with a specialist who understands the corporate foundation on which the benefit plan was built and who the plan is meant to serve means you will be better positioned to take advantage of the value they can provide and thereby save money to weather the current economy.

Hoping to be part of your New Year!

AVAILABLE BENEFITS

Choosing What's Right for Your Employees

Considering a benefit plan for your employees is significantly different than implementation.

- Where do you start with making the choice on which benefits to offer?
- Are all benefits available from all providers?
- What is the price point for those benefits, and what is involved with enacting the plan?

While benefits can play a key role in helping to attract and retain top talent, they actually protect the company, the employees and the business. The more essential reason to implement a plan is this: If you have costs, then why not incur these costs within a tax-effective structure?

Consider the purchase of a new vehicle. How nice would it be to start with the sticker price, negotiate with the salesperson and have that be the cost paid—no additional fees, levies or taxes? That is exactly what claiming health and dental expenses through a benefit plan is like.

But with so much to choose from, it is imperative to work with a specialist who can cut through the jargon to design a plan to meet the business's needs, while still being cost-effective. Not every option is right for every company, and it is up to the business owner to choose what works to match the overall business strategy for growth and sustainability.

Group benefits are a group of individual insurance options, grouped together for employees linked through their common employment. Here is a summary outline of some of the more common options available.

Life insurance is non-taxable money payable to a designated beneficiary in the event of the employee's death.

Accidental death and dismemberment (AD&D) matches the life insurance, often referred to as double indemnity because it doubles the life benefit in the event of an accidental death. There is also a portion available if the employee is dismembered in any way, and this stands outside the disability benefit.

Dependent life insurance is nontaxable insurance paid after the loss of a spouse or dependent child. Typically, the money is used to cover funeral expenses.

Short- and long-term disability are arguably the most important aspects of the benefit plan, as they provide the necessary protection of the employee's income when he or she cannot work.

Extended health care, including pharmaceutical, professional paramedical services, vision care and emergency travel assistance, is anything not covered under the provincial program that is typically covered under a benefit plan, including hearing aids, home nursing care, ambulance transport and hospital stays. All expenses are incurred in a nontaxable environment, thereby promoting a healthy workplace, which strengthens the corporate bottom line.

Dental care, which includes basic, major restorative and orthodontic work, is also non-taxable to the employees and a corporate tax deduction for the corporation. Dental insurance ensures employees maintain oral health by covering basic, major restorative or orthodontic claims.

Health spending accounts offer a non-taxable bonus for employees. Members can use the money to pay for medical or dental expenses that may not be covered by their regular plan.

Employee assistance programs provide counseling and support to help employees and their families deal with a wide range of personal and work-related issues.

The best doctors, including a professional second opinion, enable employees access to a global medical network of physicians for a second medical opinion and medical information if they or their physician suspects an illness, injury or unresolved medical condition.

Note, depending on the choices made, each type of coverage may be subject to copayments or maximums. Working with the right group benefit specialist helps to strengthen the understanding of the choices and ensure you implement a group benefits plan to meet the needs of your employees and your company.

ADMINISTRATIVE STRATEGIES

Ongoing Administration of Benefits

There are a number of areas that you need to be aware of with respect to ongoing administration of the employee benefit program. They are important because there are opportunities available that will streamline the process of managing the administrative and claim side of the program. These efficiencies will minimize the time you spend in these areas now and in the future. Not all options are available to all groups with all carriers. However, it is important to familiarize yourself with these concepts.

Direct Claims Submission by the Employee

This eliminates corporate administrative involvement at the time of submission because the employee is responsible for completion and submission of the claim(s) to the carrier for adjudication and processing.

Direct Claims Delivery to the Employee's Home

This process allows the carrier to direct the claim check(s) directly to the employee at his or her home address.

Using electronic dental claim submissions where applicable to eliminate paper forms and speed up claims payment

Many dentists are able to communicate directly with the carrier(s) to submit dental claims online. This eliminates the need for paper submission and allows earlier response for adjudication and payment.

Potential of Online Access to Claims and Administrative Information

Many carriers will allow a direct link to their mainframe so you can query their system with respect to your own information—claims status, coverage status—and this type of access can save you time corporately.

Investigate the availability of the carrier paying out-of-Canada claims directly and moving the government-sponsored claim process from the employee to the carrier.

Some carriers will accept responsibility for processing an out-of-Canada claim directly with the service provider. The employee must still submit the expense to the government-sponsored health plan. However, the government-sponsored health plan payment is now paid to the carrier. This process limits or eliminates the risk of high out-of-pocket expenses in the event of a medical emergency while traveling.

Self-Administration of the Plan May Be Appropriate

Most carriers have a software program available to allow you to administer the plan locally, on site. This would entail recording of all the administrative changes, additions and terminations, which allows you to ensure that the information is correct at all times. In addition, these systems can generate your own billing plus different types of other reports that will be of value to you.

Identify the standard waiting period for new employees before becoming eligible to join the program

Many carriers will allow different waiting periods to be applied to different benefits. Typically you are responsible for maintaining a follow-up system to ensure that the benefits are added within the defined time frame. You may wish to consider a different waiting period for dental to ensure a significant investment of employee service before incurring claim and premium expenses. This can be set up differently by employee "class."

Pay Direct Drug Card Eliminates Paper Claim Process for Drug Expenses

As described previously, the pharmacies in provinces across Canada are linked electronically with the carrier, and use of the card allows immediate, on-site adjudication in addition to limiting the out-of-pocket expenses incurred by the employee.

These are simply some areas open for discussion. The goal in providing this type of information is to develop a sense of the most efficient and effective methods of managing the internal administrative and claim processes.

BENEFITS: NEEDS VERSES WANTS

Coping with Entitlement

Right or wrong, no entrepreneur believes his company is a bad place to work. But does your company really deliver what today's best employees want?

Does your company do the following?

1. Offer work or a product that creates excitement, pride and a sense of accomplishment among employees.
2. Communicate frequently, honestly and openly about the business with employees.
3. Provide clear direction on how individuals and groups contribute to the business.
4. Acknowledge a job well done with fair bonuses (at least 5 percent of salary), awards or simple thank-yous.
5. Solicit and, when appropriate, act on employee suggestions.
6. Offer salaries and benefits that are competitive with those of people in similar roles at other companies.
7. Clearly communicate opportunities for advancement, and employ a fair selection process.
8. Educate employees on how they can receive greater compensation.
9. Reside in an easily accessible location close to popular amenities.
10. Offer job flexibility in the form of customized work hours, job sharing, reduced workweeks, sabbatical programs and telecommuting.

Health Care Benefits—Part of a Wish List or Need?

Analyzing out-of-pocket expense versus premium dollars does not always add up. Let's look at some alarming statistics that will help not only motivate a closer look at the value of these benefits as part of the financial plan but also create an understand of the need.

Statistics

Twenty-eight percent of all Canadians still believe all medical and hospital bills will be paid for by provincial health plans.

Fifty-one percent of all Canadians have group insurance plans.[1]

The average healthy family spends $1,508 annually toward drugs, dental and extended health care not covered by the provincial plan. This excludes any expense incurred for holistic treatments and over-the-counter drugs or vitamins purchased, which is a growing trend in society among baby boomers.

The average expense for a self-employed average baby boomer looking for health-care coverage with a plan offering unlimited health-care coverage and drug coverage, paramedical coverage, private nursing, vision care, hearing aids, critical illness, $5 million of out-of-province coverage and dental coverage monthly is as follows:

Single	$125.11
Couple	$211.57
Family	$295.22[2]

Buyer beware of lower monthly premiums, as there are sure to be limits within drug, dental and extended health that may not meet long-term needs. With more and more expensive drugs coming into the market, it pays to purchase a plan without any limitations on drugs. Getting diagnosed with a very common illness such as diabetes will exhaust the plan in a very short period of time.

---

[1] Desjardin Financial Security National Health Survey.
[2] Alberta Blue Cross—rates.

Once a plan with a limit on drugs has reached its maximum limit for drugs, you will be forced to search for a new benefits provider who will not cover your preexisting condition.

Other Statistics

Forty-three percent of all Canadians aged 35 to 65 have no RRSPs.[3]

Seventy percent of Canadian entrepreneurs own RRSPs compared to 55 percent of paid employees, and 42 percent of small business owners aged 18 to 34 plan to use RRSPs to finance their retirement versus 35 percent of these aged 50 to 64.

---

[3] BBM RTS Canada Fall.

THE INSANITY WHEEL

Get off the Treadmill

Everyone in business knows the old adage of insanity: continually doing the same thing and expecting different results.

The same applies to employee group benefits.

Time after time, employers will get fed up with their current benefit plan, the benefit options provided and especially the pricing. However, instead of looking for something different, something to stop the cycle, they typically change only the carrier or the broker.

So what has been accomplished in this scenario?

Either the existing broker or a new broker has come into the picture and suggested that pricing can be established with a new insurance carrier where the company can get better pricing with no loss of coverage. Someone convinces the owner it's a good deal, and typically, employers go for it, saving around 10 to 12 percent over the existing rates. Inevitability, times marches on, and once again, the pricing has gone up, and the cycle recommences because there has been no real change made on the benefit plan. There is no analysis of what caused the cycle.

In essence, nothing changes as the business owner has enacted the same old strategy but expected different results.

It can be different with the introduction of strategy, analysis and planning.

A good plan analysis will review the existing plan design and measure it against the overall business strategy of the company. Review the past history of the benefit costs and claims measure results and account for the money being spent on claims and compare it the money being spent to provide the coverage in the first place. This ensures the owner knows all of the ins and outs of the package and how everything is working and will be able to compare it to how it is actually working. With the methodology that a benefit plan should mirror the business plan, being just as fluid and changeable as the business over time, achieving this removes the client from the hamster wheel.

Look at what is important to the plan members, understand the pricing, ensure catastrophic events are covered and then plan and implement strategic solutions, which will ensure superior coverage and price stability over time so the cycle is stopped in its tracks. The insanity is over.

CHOICE AND CONTROL

Building Better Benefits

What goes into designing the perfect benefit plan?

Everyone's definition of this is different depending upon many circumstances.

Perfection would have to suit everyone's needs as well as satisfy their wants. A program should be built to appeal to the complexities of the work force, within the right price index to meet the requirements of the business owner to be sustainable over the long term.

Let's not forget flexible, tax effective and, above all else, easy to administer, understand, and use. If, at the end of the day, employees can't get the claims paid, what's the use?

Sounds like a Health-Care Spending Account (HSA)

Health spending accounts have been around and actively used for more than a quarter of a century; however, it is only the last few years that the concept has taken off as mainstream.

Health spending accounts provide a cost-effective way to provide coverage for health services, such as paramedical professionals in chiropractic, physiotherapy, massage, acupuncture, etc., as well as vision care, including laser eye surgery and dental services, including implants, to name a few. A self-funded option 100 percent paid for by the employer is budgetable, whereby the overall maximum is defined by classification, not by service, thereby leaving the end user able to make the decision on how he or she wants to spend his or her allotted dollars according to his or her own needs.

Choice and control, what a novel idea!

Survey after survey of human resource professions indicate employees recognize the health spending accounts to be a valuable part of their overall benefit strategy.

Aside from the tax advantages to the employer and ease of use for the employees, health spending accounts fit easily within the program, forming the mortar for the brick is solid coverage for any company—of any size.

With defined maximums, the benefit itself becomes a budgetable expense, easy to predict and plan for from one year to the next. For instance (keeping the number low and round), if an employer has ten employees and offers a health spending account at $1,000 per employee, then the total exposure for the employer is the $10,000 maximum usage, plus the administration fees, which are charged on claims only. And that number doesn't change from year to year, unless the employer changes it.

A health spending account is flexible enough to be used in conjunction with a traditional benefit plan, topping up for those expenses that are not covered under typical insured plans. An example would be an employee who uses chiropractic services on a regular basis, and his or her base plan provides for $500 per practitioner per person per year. For someone utilizing these services on a regular basis, it is not hard to exceed the $500, but if one has a health spending account to top up the extra expenses, then that employee, who doesn't use the other benefits, is now receiving benefits the employer intended.

Health spending accounts encourage employees to be good consumers while at the same time providing them with what everyone wants at the end of the day: choice and control.

BEING FLEXIBLE

Building Benefits to Suit Everyone

It is difficult to find a benefit plan to suit everyone's needs as well as satisfy everyone's wants—a plan that not only appeals to the employees but also is within the right price index to meet the requirements of the employer and be sustainable over the long term.

Let's not forget that the benefit plan should be flexible, tax effective and, above all else, easy to understand and use, because let's face it: If you can't get the claims paid, what's the use?

That sounds like a health-care spending account.

Health spending accounts have been around and actively used for more than a quarter of a century; however, it is only in the last few years that the concept has become mainstream.

Health spending accounts provide a cost effective way to provide coverage for pharmaceutical, health services, such as professionals in chiropractic, physiotherapy, massage, acupuncture, etc., as well as vision care, including laser eye surgery and dental services, including implants, whereby the overall maximum is defined by user, not by service, thereby leaving the end users—the employees—able to make the decision on how they want to spend their allotted dollars according to their own needs.

Aside from the tax advantages to the employer and ease of use for the employees, health spending accounts fit easily within the planning strategy of any company, of any size. The maximum benefits are defined, and the benefit itself becomes a budgetable expense that is easy to predict and plan for from one year to the next. For instance (keeping the number low and round), if an employer has ten employees and offers a health spending account at $1,000 per employee, then the total exposure for the employer is the $10,000 maximum usage, plus the administration fees, which are charged on claims only. That number doesn't change from year to year unless the employer changes it.

A health spending account is flexible enough to be used in conjunction with a traditional benefit plan, topping up for those expenses that are not covered under typical insured plans.

A health spending account encourages employees to be good consumers while at the same time providing them with what everyone wants at the end of the day: choice and control.

WHAT YOU DON'T KNOW

Fact: You Simply Don't Know What You Don't Know

That is why we treat every renewal as an opportunity to earn the business all over again. The renewal provides an opportunity to analyze and conduct a thorough review of the insurance or benefit provider's underwriting methods to ensure their basis for establishing the renewal rates is rational and in line with marketplace standards. Where appropriate negotiations are initiated to secure a fair renewal based on current plan design, applicable experience results and insured employee demographics.

Insured Pooled Benefits

The insured pooled benefits are underwritten and administered through an insurance underwriter. When these benefits are referred to as pooled, it means the carrier blends your plan results with other policyholders for the purpose of assessing premiums and claims experience. Pricing of the pooled benefits is not typically impacted by your own experience unless the plan results are significantly above the statistical norm.

Benefits that fall under this category are life insurance, accidental death and dismemberment, dependent life, critical illness and long-term disability.

Pooling these categories of insurance is the most economical approach to pricing this type of benefit because the claims are typically for large amounts, infrequent and difficult to predict. Pooling simply moves the entire risk for experience results to the insured carrier. The factors that most impact the development of the pooled benefit rate are the employee demographics (age, gender and occupation), including the following:

- average age of the group's members as a whole
- how many current employees are insured under the plan
- change in the number of covered employees since last year
- insured experience-rated benefits

Experience-rated benefits under an insured plan are underwritten and administered through an underwriter. These benefits are priced based, to a certain percentage, on a company's own usage of these benefits. While a good loss ratio will contribute to a favourable renewal, additional cost factors must also be considered when calculating renewal rates. These factors can include the following:

i. Inflation
ii. Provincial cost downloading and funding changes
iii. Canada's aging workforce
iv. A rise in the volume and cost of prescription drug expenditures
v. Newer, more complex and more expensive treatments and services
vi. Dental fee guides
vii. The IBNR

Self-Insured Benefits

The self-insured benefits, administrative services only (ASO), health-care spending accounts (HSA) can be provided and administered through an insurance underwriter under the same umbrella as the insured benefits or provided through a separate benefit company. These benefits are funded 100 percent by company corporate dollars where an administration fee is paid based on usage only. There is no payroll deduction to the employee for these benefits. Cost sharing is designed in the copayment—pay at the counter portion of the plan.

BUILDING THE UNIQUE

Adding a Health Spending Account

With all that business owners have to choose from when building their employee benefit program, there is nothing more practical or flexible than a health-care spending account (HSA).

A HSA can be made to fit within the existing benefit plan like a glove, or it can be designed to work as a full-on account from which employees draw the funds necessary to pay their health and dental claims—tax free. As an add-on, or a top-up, a HSA offers flexibility of choice of coverage options employees crave, while at the same time creating cost stability for employers in predicting and budgeting for their limited benefit dollars.

A well-designed benefit plan will often include a HSA option as a sound business investment. A health spending account not only works to attain the goal of attracting and retaining employees but can actually make the difference between an employee choosing a competitor over the existing employer because of the flexibility of the plan. Imagine employees' delight when they learn their benefit program provides funding for a private MRI not typically covered under the traditional portion of the plan. Employers must understand they have control over what to budget for the coming year and stick to that budget, knowing any amount not used by the employee is money not lost to the company.

Creating a plan to mesh a HSA with a traditional style plan will create the assurance of superior coverage. Work-life balance means the ability of the employee to pay for the services specific to their family needs, not just what the book says is available for coverage.

For instance, many plans include coverage for:

- 80 percent prescriptions
- $500 for paramedical services (chiro, massage, physio, etc.)
- $200 every 24 months for vision
- 80 percent basic dental (filling, extractions, regular maintenance)
- 50 percent major restorative (crowns, dentures, bridges)

But what about services that fall outside this coverage?

A health spending account allows the employer to stipulate how much to offer the employee; use $500 as an example, where the employee can fill in the gaps of coverage for themselves.

The employer knows their liability for the HSA is $500 (cost stability) per employee.

The employee can use the additional $500 where he or she needs it most, whether it's picking up the additional 20 percent for prescriptions or additional glasses coverage, even additional orthodontic, which may not even appear on the traditional plan.

And remember, a health spending account forms part of the overall strategy. A well-designed benefit plan will be able to meet the corporate budgeting needs, as well as the claiming needs of the employees with the purpose of creating a unique plan to mirror the corporate compensation philosophy over the long term.

PROPER COMMUNICATION

Education Matters

As a Canadian employer, making a group benefit program available to employees is a must. But even more important is information—telling them about the program and its value.

How benefit plan information is presented depends on a number of things, including the corporate culture and employee population. Whether a company is paying the whole premium or sharing the bill with employees, individuals who understand the coverage are more likely to appreciate the plan and to work in partnership to keep it affordable for the long run.

Studies show that companies with the best track record educating employees typically saw a seven percent premium increase, while companies facing higher increases—a medium of 17 percent—did less to help workers make cost-effective decisions. This 10 percent difference is hard to ignore. Employers who ensure employees understand how coverage works best for the long term are reaping the rewards.

Explaining benefits not only ensures people understand what is covered, but it also avoids disappointments down the road, where people assume incorrectly that a product or service is covered. Education means employees appreciate the benefits provided and the expenses paid on their behalf. It also establishes that although group benefits are valuable, they are not free.

For many workers with young families, prescription medication coverage might be of greatest interest, but it's also worthwhile to talk about the importance of other benefits, such as life, accidental death and dismemberment, short- and long-term disability or critical illness. After all, it's one thing to help a family pay for medications they need. It's another to help pay all the family's bills through income replacement if a breadwinner can't work because of an illness or accident. Every client of ours has a custom benefit plan, not an off-the-shelf program. Successful plans include features like deductibles and copayments. These directly involve employees in every purchase, reminding them to ensure each purchase is appropriate. This also encourages what the medical community calls compliance. This means patients follow the doctor's instruction, like taking medications for the full period prescribed, not just until they initially feel better. This kind of smart consumer behavior helps ensure the treatment is successful and avoids repeat visits to the doctor to start the treatment process over again, often with a new prescription. Choice is critical to managing the rising costs of benefits.

A benefit plan typically starts with basic group life insurance for employees. This can be based on a flat amount (i.e., $25,000 or a percentage of salary). There is also income replacement (short- and long-term disability income). There are critical illness options, plus decisions to make about prescription drugs, health, dental and vision benefits. Although health, dental and drugs are among the most popular, prescription drugs can account for the largest portion of the plan's premium, so you'll want to consider your options carefully.

Having options gives increased control over the cost, today and tomorrow. And at each review, it is important to explore benefit options as a plan set in force today may not meet the needs of the company five years down the road. Yearly reviews ensure that the company is never paying for benefits not wanted or missing coverage's thought to be included.

FUNDING SHAREHOLDERS

It's Only Paper until the Funding Is Provided

- Does your shareholder agreement have specific sections that deal with partner dissatisfaction, partner death and partner disability?
- Has the disability section of your shareholder agreement been properly integrated with your group or corporate disability program?
- Do you have proper shareholder agreement funding for death and disability? (Many corporations have life insurance in place in the event of a shareholder death. However, many corporations have not resolved the funding requirements for a shareholder disability.) Have you?
- Do you have proper funding in place for a partnership disability buyout in the event that a shareholder suffers a severe and prolonged disability?
- Have you explored a wage loss replacement plan to see if your corporation would be eligible for this taxable but corporately paid benefit?
- Does your group insurance program conflict with your shareholder agreement? Are you paying disability premiums for benefits you will not be able to collect?
- Does your shareholder agreement contain specifics on how the valuation of your business will be determined? Do your life insurance and disability insurance contracts reflect the current valuation of your business?

- Does your shareholder agreement specifically state how long a shareholder will continue to receive a salary from the corporation if he or she becomes sick or hurt?
- What definition is used in your shareholder agreement to define a disability? Has a third party been appointed to adjudicate possible claims?
- If you have funded your shareholder agreement with life insurance, have you been shown the advantages of universal life policies over term policies? If you currently have term insurance policies, are they convertible to universal life policies?

Section 4

THE END USER
ALL ABOUT THE EMPLOYEE

EMPLOYEE EXPECTATION

What Do Employees Want?

It is no secret employee group benefit plans provide a substantial financial advantage to employees who benefit per their own workplace or via a spousal program. Though offering benefits is not legally required of employers, according to a 2016 Sun Life Financial Study, about three-quarters of Canadian employees believe they are entitled to benefits.

As a result, more than half of the respondents reported to be experiencing one or more serious health issues:

- 29 percent say they have experienced a mental health issue such as debilitating stress, anxiety, depression or substance abuse
- 16 percent have a chronic or degenerative condition, such as diabetes, multiple sclerosis or Alzheimer's
- 12 percent had a serious accident
- 10 percent experienced a serious health event, such as a stroke, heart attack or cancer
- 2 percent have received a terminal illness diagnosis

Within this segment of respondents, 42 percent said these conditions have impacted them financially.

Without access to a well-designed benefit plan, employees may go without the coverage they require and suffer mentally, physically and financially as a result, or they may seek employment elsewhere where benefits are provided.

Alternatively, those employers not providing benefits may be turning their back on an excellent tax deduction for their corporation.

Health and dental benefits in Canada, outside the province of Quebec, are considered nontaxable, and all premiums paid by an employer toward employee group benefits are considered a corporate tax deduction.

FROM GOOD TO GREAT

Benefits to Attract and Retain Employees

Good benefits are a factor of remunerations employees have come to expect in any organization worth their consideration for employment. Great benefits are options and choice components, which actually make an impact on employees' perspective of where they work and what kind of employer they have.

In today's diverse and fluctuating economy, businesses of all sizes and in all markets have come to recognize their most valuable assets to be their employees and the tax effectiveness of the employee group benefit plan. Many companies distinguish themselves by fostering strong relationships, engaging employees at the individual level and looking out for the employees' personal needs as ways to attract and preserve high-caliber people in their organizations.

Employees know they are a valuable asset to a business and how that value increases the longer they stay. As the economy begins to pick up, so will competitive job offers to tempt employees away. More than position itself, many factors influence a worker's decision to stay or move on.

With a focus on family and well-being, many consider the impacts of total compensation as key factors in whether or not to stay. Compensation includes not only wages or salary but also what the company can offer in benefits, vacation and lifestyle prerequisites, such as flexible hours, accommodation of family needs and so on.

With employee benefits, companies are looking for the most cost-effective solutions to provide the coverage their workers want. One great way to offer employees cost-effective, comprehensive benefits is to top up with a health spending account.

What's a Health Spending Account (HSA)?

There is not a plan out there that can meet everyone's expectations of a benefit plan, but with a well-designed health spending account, employers only provide more benefits for employees but provide the most important thing for these savvy shoppers—choice in care and provider services, as well as control over how they spend their money for these services.

Unlike a more traditional style of plan, a HSA is not an insurance product. HSAs are fully funded by the employer and administered by a benefits provider to the overall set maximum.

Without question, HSAs are cost effective, with no sign-up fees, no transaction fees and no medical questionnaires to answer. The administrative fee is applied on claims only.

While HSAs are designed to suit the needs of employees and their families, they also provide tax advantages for employers and employees alike. The employee receives the compensation on claims tax free, and the employer receives a corporate tax deduction for the premium, plus the administration fees to provide the coverage.

Always check with your accountant for tax advice.

ACCURATE ENROLLMENTS

Plan Member Data

Plan member data is information used to determine the amount of benefit coverage plan members are entitled to receive. This information is also used to calculate the group's monthly premiums. Receiving and maintaining accurate data is critical to your insurance carrier's ability to provide the best hassle-free coverage.

To assist in this task, review the following checklist periodically to ensure all essential plan member data requirements are being met for your group.

Date of hire: This is the first day the employee began work. When enrolling members, the date of hire is used to determine the waiting period found in many group benefit plans. The waiting period is a period of continuous active employment, as shown in the benefit schedule, following which the plan member becomes eligible for insurance.

Eligibility: Some plans require employees to work a minimum of 25 hours per week to qualify for insurance.

Enrollment: Plans with mandatory participation require all eligible employees to enroll for benefits. (However, if similar coverage exists elsewhere, health and dental benefits may be waived.)

Earnings: Late earnings updates result in incorrect premium billing and possible reductions to disability and salary-related life insurance benefits.

Employee classification: Plans determine benefit levels and qualifications by employee class. Typical classes include "owner," "management," or "all other employees." Each classification has different benefit levels, risk assessment and enrollment criteria.

Occupation description: Occupation descriptions are important to the calculation of premiums for each enrolled member. Changes to job title should be communicated to the insurance carrier as soon as they occur.

Termination: Promptly notify your insurance carrier of all terminated employees and their last effective date of employment. When terminations are not reported, premiums continue to be collected, and ineligible persons may claim benefits to which they are not entitled.

Enrollments

Plan members' enrollment (or reenrollment) application for group benefit coverage is to be completed on the date of hire or rehire. Where required, the form must be signed no later than 31 days after the plan member's first day of eligibility and promptly submitted to the insurance carrier.

If participation is non-mandatory, the plan member seeking benefits will be considered a late applicant when the above requirement is not met and the following conditions affect late applicants.

Coverage not guaranteed: Coverage for late applicants is not guaranteed. The insurance carrier has the right to approve or decline coverage based on evidence submitted, as well as the right to request additional evidence of insurability information.

Extra costs: The late applicant bears the cost of extra medical information required to assess insurability.

Limitations on dental: In the case of dental benefits, coverage will be limited to a set dollar amount as outlined in the contract for the first 12 months of coverage.

Coverage only effective when approved: Coverage will only begin when written approval is granted by the insurance carrier.

When a plan member fails to properly enroll in a plan with mandatory participation, the situation can only be corrected by manually backdating records, which is a costly and inefficient process.

THE LATE APPLICANT

Medical Underwriting and Evidence of Insurability

Most of the time, group health plan members don't have to pass a medical examination or take any special tests to qualify for insurance coverage under the group plan.

In some cases, medical evidence has to be completed. Groups generally have non-evidence limits in their contracts, whether it is for the long- or short-term disability benefits or the life and accidental death and dismemberment benefits.

When benefit amounts are salary-based, if a member's salary qualifies for an amount of life or long-term disability benefit volume that is over the non-evidence limit, the member must complete an evidence of insurability form to qualify for the increased coverage.

When the plan members or dependents have not applied for benefits within the time outlined in the contract, these applicants are considered late and are required to submit an evidence of insurability form.

Most contracts with employee optional and spousal optional life benefits require a completed evidence of insurability form. An exception may be when optional life is transferred from a prior carrier.

Regarding other forms required, with applications for employee optional life or spousal optional life, an optional life application form or a cover letter outlining the coverage being requested is required. The cover letter must include the benefits being applied for, the volume of coverage according to the contract and the plan member or dependent's name. The cover letter is most likely to be used by plan sponsors of self-administered plans.

In a late-applicant situation, most insurance carriers require the applicant for enrollment or change form.

Plan members are considered late applicants if one of the following applies:

- they apply for coverage under the group benefit program later than the limitation in the contract (e.g., 31 days after the date in which they or their dependents are first eligible), or
- they refuse or cancel coverage under the group benefits program and then reapply at a later date.

Next, let's discuss medical underwriting. With plans that are non-mandatory, the plan administrator asks employees about benefit coverage when they join the company. Some will say yes, and others will say no. If an employee says no at first and yes at a later date, that individual is considered a late applicant, and underwriting will screen the applicant. The applicant may have refused the insurance and then discovered a need for coverage related to an illness or condition.

At this point, the insurance carrier may choose to gather additional information from the applicant's doctor to see if there are any medical conditions. The medical underwriting area does this background work to manage antiselection risks and keep the cost of the plan reasonable for all employers and their employees.

To avoid late applicants, consider the following options:

- use Internet enrollment (if available),
- complete the enrollment form at employee orientation,
- send in new forms at the time the change occurs.

THE SHIFT IN THE CANADIAN WORKFORCE

Not only are Canadian workers getting older, but there is also a distinct shift the types of workers being employed. According to Statistics Canada, for the first time ever, there are now more people age 65 and over than there are under 15.

With these changes, it is no surprise that Canadian employers are hiring a broad variety of nontraditional workers (i.e., contract, consultant, remote or freelance), a trend likely to accelerate over the next decade. With the younger workforce rethinking their approach to employment, employers are changing the way they consider fulfilling their staffing needs. Technology has enabled people to work wherever they are and throws the old nine-to-five punch clock in the bin designed to hold all things now considered outdated and archaic.

Consider what these new technologies and attitudes toward employment will result in as we look out into the not-too-distant future of employment. What impact will this have on the benefit plan? Creative and changeable benefits aimed at adapting to these changing needs of the workforce will be paramount, remembering a plan built today should be not a set-it and leave-it plan. The plan should be as changeable as the business plan, as adaptable as the workforce hired to take that business into a successful future.

COMPLIANCE ISN'T OPTIONAL

Benefits for the Long Term

There are always a lot of questions when it comes to implementing or sustaining a benefit plan, not least of which are employees wanting to opt out of the entire coverage. This is often a bone of contention when the question of liability comes into play. The role of the broker is to ensure the corporation is informed, and the purpose of insurance is to mitigate risk. Just because something hasn't happened so far doesn't mean it won't. Put another way, compliance and liability risks are never a risk, until they are.

Claims are increasing as a result of negligence on benefit issues. Here is a brief highlight of some of the most common liability issues.

Extending Coverage upon Termination of Employment

The minimum notice period applicable to all employees is found within the Employment Standards Act, 2000. The length of these periods is based upon the employee's years of service with the employer. Under the act, employers are required to provide a minimum period of salary continuance and benefit coverage as the employee is deemed to be actively at work.

Most employee benefit plans are set so the coverage terminates on the date of termination. Some employers negotiate continuation of benefits after the termination as part of the severance agreement; however, some benefits, like long-term disability, are not eligible to be continued after termination because the employee would not be deemed to be actively at work in the event of a disability claim.

Accurate Description of Employee Benefits

Employers have an obligation to describe the extent of employee benefit coverage accurately. Liability issues come up when the booklet inaccurately describes the terms of the policy from the insurance company, and where an employer misrepresents the nature of benefits in an offer of employment or a contract of employment. An employee has a claim for the benefit coverage stated in the contract regardless of the terms of the actual benefits policy. If the terms of the policy are not the same as those represented by the employer, the employer may face liability for the coverage described in the contract of employment

An employer's failure to pay premiums for benefit coverage may lead to liability far in excess of the value of those premiums. Once an employer has represented to its employees that it is providing certain benefit programs, those programs must be provided. If they are cancelled because of the employer's failure to pay premiums, an employee may have a claim against the employer for all of the benefits it would have received had that premium been paid.

Negligence in Administering Benefit Policies

The benefit policy is placed under corporation's name for the benefit of the employees. The employee's do not own this policy. Employers administer the benefit plan on behalf of the insurer. As such, they deliver policy booklets to employees assist in the completion of applications and claim forms and collect premiums via payroll deductions.

Insurers and employees may be jointly and severally liable for any errors or omissions that occur in the administration of benefit plans. Traditionally, insurers could only recover a small amount from employers who were negligent in the administration of benefit plans. Recovery in such cases was limited to the premiums that the insurer had not paid. However, the law now allows insurers to claim indemnification from employers. It is also possible that employees administering benefit plans on behalf of their employer may find themselves personally liable for errors in administering benefit plans where they fail to obtain appropriate insurance coverage or fail to properly report a claim.

Vested Rights

Even the cancellation of benefit plans can raise a number of liability issues when it pertains to the expectation of benefits by the employees. Take for example if an employee made appointments with the expectation of coverage, only to learn the coverage was terminated without notice and they are now responsible for those expenses.

Human Rights Code

The Human Rights Code prohibits discrimination in employment based upon race, ancestry, place of origin, color, ethnic origin, citizenship, creed, sex, sexual orientation, gender identity, gender expression, age, record of offenses, marital status, same-sex partnership status, family status and disability.

As the cost of benefit coverage increases, many insurance companies and employers are looking at ways of controlling costs by limiting the type of benefit coverage provided. This is especially true in the case of drug plans. Increasingly these plans are limiting the types of drugs that will be paid for by the plan. These limitations have not yet been challenged in Canada, but they have been in the United States. One can see that it is only a matter of time before employees challenge their insurer (and their employer) because a policy does not cover certain treatments for these disabilities.

Fiduciary Obligations

Employers have also been found liable for failure to bring the terms of benefit policies to the attention of their employees. An example is when an employee is terminated and not told he or she has 31 days to convert his or her life insurance or disability coverage into an individual policy.

Court proceedings have found that as a result the death of a former employee, the employer was liable to the employee's estate when he died during the notice period. In another situation, the employer was liable—breach of duty—to the employee in negligence on the basis that it owed a duty to the employee to assist him in completing forms for LTD benefits.

As the relationship between employers and employees become more complex, we can expect to see increasing obligations being placed upon employers toward their employees. Compliance is not an option. In the field of employee benefits, employers are expected to administer the benefit plans fairly, accurately and efficiently. A failure to do so may lead to liability far in excess of the cost of providing the appropriate benefit coverage.

ENROLLMENT REQUIREMENTS

Health Care Requirements

Health care not a sexy conversation but essential knowledge nonetheless. For instance, did you know before a plan member (employee) can be eligible to be on the benefit plan, he or she must be covered by his or her provincial health-care plan?

This information is valuable if your company hires temporary foreign workers.

Extended health care provided under a private group insurance plan is meant to supplement coverage provided under a publicly funded provincial or federal health-care plan. In this way, plan members have financial assistance for many of their regular and catastrophic medical expenses from both the public plan and their private group insurance plan.

From time to time, insurance carriers are made aware via an out-of-Canada medical emergency claim that an employee doesn't have provincial health-care coverage in place but is nonetheless enrolled under an employer-sponsored extended health care program. To be eligible for coverage, plan members must be continuously covered under a provincial or federal health-care plan.

Insurance carriers need to be notified if employees are listed for coverage under the benefit plan yet are not actively covered by their provincial or federal plan or had coverage that's lapsed. In this event, their extended health care coverage should be discontinued. They are eligible for all other benefits.

Please note, if there is an employee who is in the waiting period for his or her provincial plan but has not yet qualified for coverage, many insurance providers have options for coverage until he or she is approved and can join the regular plan.

EMPLOYEES WAIVING COVERAGE

What Benefits Employees Can Waive?

A confusing point on any benefit plan is employees' ability to waive off benefits when they have alternate coverage.

A basic benefit plan will include life insurance, accidental death and dismemberment, dependent life insurance, long and short-term disability, pharmacy, extended health care, professional paramedical services, vision and dental care. On a typical mandatory benefit plan, an employee must be enrolled for the life, AD&D, dependent life (if they have dependents) and short- and long-term disability. Employees can waive the pharmacy, health, professional paramedical, vision and dental care only when they have spousal coverage elsewhere. These are the only benefits provided to both the employee and his or her family members.

In the same manner, a business owner will not provide insured coverage for the spouse of an employee (nonemployee) wage at the time of his or her death or disability, nor will another employer provide insured coverage for your employee.

Allowing an employee to completely decline all benefit coverage has serious ramifications for employees, their families and, ultimately, the company for which they are employed. Please refer to an employment or corporate lawyer for further liability details.

Let's use an example of an employee who has declined full coverage assuming, he or she was completely covered for health and dental under his or her spouse. Now the spouse has lost coverage for one reason or another, and the employee wants to be on this benefit plan. The insurance carrier will not allow this without all family members completing an evidence of insurability questionnaire. The insured underwriter reserves the right to decline coverage. If all members of the family are approved for coverage, some of the benefits approved will still have first-year limitations.

Let's take this same scenario one step further and assume the same employee who declined this coverage incurs a disability. What now? This employee has no ability to replace his or her wage as he or she assumed that he or she was covered under the spouse's plan. It's unlikely the employee will approach the spouse's employer; however, he or she may approach his or her own employer and request coverage.

As they are already the car wreck in the middle of the intersection, as the saying goes, no coverage will be available to this employee.

Perhaps they will claim that they didn't understand what they were waiving and now need the funds to sustain a quality of life. At that point, what would stop the employee from pursuing the issue legally to seek a settlement?

The same scenario applies to the employee's beneficiary in the event of his or her death and there is no other coverage in place.

Bottom line, the employee should have been listed for coverage. There should have been insured coverage in place for this employee in the event of a catastrophic situation.

Providing benefits to an employee group demands 100 percent participation from all of your employees. It's the difference between price and cost—the price of premiums versus the cost of liability charges.

TELEPHONE PRE-SCREENING QUESTIONS

Contributed from Alison McMahon, Twofold

Pre-screening allows the employer to determine if the candidate's qualifications, experience, workplace preferences and salary expectations are in line with the position and organization. Pre-screening is typically done over the phone, saving time and eliminating unlikely candidates.

In a pre-screen, interviewers would typically ask basic questions that allow them to eliminate candidates who do not fit the job requirements and working conditions, leaving more suited candidates to pursue. Common questions include:

- Interest in the job—ensuring they have a genuine interest in the job.
    - What interested you about the position?
    - What do you know about our company?
- Availability—ensuring their availability matches the required schedule for the position.
    - What is your availability like?
    - Our typical working hours are _____. Does this work for your schedule?
- Salary—ensuring their salary expectations are in line with what is being offered.
    - What are your salary expectations for this position?
    - What is the minimum salary you'd consider to accept a new position?

- Location—ensuring the location is convenient and if they have to commute that it will not cause them hardship.
  ◦ Our business is located _____. Will that work for you?
  ◦ Is this a reasonable commute?

In addition to these questions, you want to review their resume to make sure there aren't any major gaps in employment. You want to also consider the length of employment in previous positions. Do they have a history of staying with a company or jumping around? Remember, past behaviors can help predict future patterns.

Depending on the position and the amount of information that is desired, additional position-specific questions can be asked. The pre-screen should not be too lengthy, typically no more than 15 minutes.

PRIVACY

Understanding the Privacy Legislation

January 1, 2004, will mark the day the Personal Information Protection and Electronic Documents Act (PIPEDA) will become law. This new law will affect employers, insurers and providers in connection with their commercial activities across Canada. Once passed, this legislation will also dictate how we can collect, use and disclose plan members' personal information.

PIPEDA contains a set of rules for collecting, using and disclosing personal information.

Use refers to the treatment and handling of personal information.

Disclosure refers to making personal information available to others.

Consent refers to the voluntary agreement with what is being done or proposed. This can be expressed either verbally or by a signature or simply implied.

Personal information includes any factual or subjective information, recorded or not, about an identifiable individual. Example: age, name, ID number, income, ethnic origin, blood type, social status, employee files, credit records, loan records, medical records. Personal information does not include the name, title, business address or telephone number of an employee.

In order to comply with federal and provincial privacy laws, as it applies to the group benefit plan, plan administrators will no longer be permitted to pre-screen applicants' health statements since they contain sensitive personal and medical information. Instead, members should send health statements directly to the insurance carrier's medical underwriting department for processing.

Consent

From now on the insurance community will not disclose sensitive personal information such as financial or medical information about an individual without the plan member's express written or verbal consent. This would include information such as diagnosis, drug type or DIN, number of claims made or bank account information, for example.

Verbal consent by phone will require that the caller provide sufficient information to allow the insurance carrier to authenticate him or her as the member. Other, more general types of information may be released with the member's implied consent. We require the caller to provide enough information to assure us that the member has authorized the inquiry.

The insurance carrier will provide information about a member's current claim, with the implied consent of the member. This would include information such as whether the claim has been received and processed, reasons for claims decision (for example, the claim was submitted late or service is not covered under the plan) and date of payment. When a call is made regarding the member but not by the member him- or herself, the plan administrator will be asked for details such as the member's name, certificate and policy number. The plan administrator should know enough detail about the issue to demonstrate that the member has authorized the administrator to call in on his or her behalf.

For information on past claims, claim details or more sensitive personal information, such as financial or medical information, the member's express consent is required.

The act is based upon ten fair information principles, and these include the following.

Accountability

Appoint an individual responsible for an organization's compliance. This means this person must protect personal information held by the organization or processed by a third party.

Identifying Purposes

Reasons why the information is being collected and the purpose before and at the time of collection. New purposes require new consent.

Obtain Consent

Knowledge and consent are required for collection, use and disclosure. The nature of the consent given (expressed versus implied) depends on the sensitivity of the information. For example, expressed consent should be used whenever possible in all cases when the personal information is considered sensitive. Medical information is always considered sensitive.

Limiting Collection

Limit the collection of personal information to what is necessary. This will reduce the risk of inappropriate use and disclosure of the information. Always clearly explain why the information is necessary.

Limiting Use, Disclosure and Retention

As with the above, limit not only what is collected, but what is disclosed. Destroy personal information when it is no longer necessary, like when an employee is no longer employed.

Accuracy

Ensure that personal information is correct, complete and up to date.

Safeguards

Ensure information is secured from loss, theft or wrongful disclosure, such as intruders being able to steal garbage and view personal information on clients and personnel. The greater the sensitivity, the greater the safeguards whereby physical, technological and organizational controls should be implemented.

Openness

Ensure the members understand what the privacy laws mean to them.

Individual Access

Upon request, inform a member of the existence, use and disclosure of their personal information and provide access to this information.

Challenging Compliance (Provide Recourse)

Organizations should have procedures in place to deal with members' complaints regarding privacy issues.

THE IMPACT OF DOWNSIZING

Employee Participation and Pricing

The Impact of Reduced Employee Participation and the Renewal

For the last two years, employers have been left holding the bag, as it were, for employees no longer covered under a benefit plan. Though it is true, fewer employees on a benefit plan reduces the premium costs. But what about the impact of this reduction at renewal time?

Remember, employee group benefits are like one-year term insurance and are repriced annually. In the year previous, employers had a set number of employees and the usage was patterned accordingly, almost predictably. The insured benefits were priced based upon the number of participants, their average age and the male-to-female split, and when there was consistency, year over year, these rates likely fluctuated perhaps 3 to 5 percent annually, or often resulted in little to no change. Accounting for about two-thirds of the premium dollars, health and dental benefits, by contrast, are priced according to covered options and usage—trend, inflation, credibility and weighting.

When the bust of the economy started to take hold and employees anticipated layoff or were let go, the first thing the majority did was access all they could of the employee benefit program and use them to their maximums prior to leaving. As an entitlement factor, these benefits were non-taxable income to be used according to coverage maximums allowable. And though the rates did not change immediately, once the plan was reevaluated by the insurance carrier and claims, in many cases, amounted to almost double what was paid in premium, rates had to be increased. With the experience ratios incredibly high and a significantly reduced number of covered members to foot the bill, this left many employers questioning whether to continue the benefits or not.

Though we all want something for nothing, that is not the case—ever. An insurance carrier is no different than any other business. When it comes to claims, they need to have the funds available to cover the usage, especially on the day-to-day choice benefits, such as dental, vision care and paramedical services, such as massage therapy. In order to plan where a plan is to go in the future, it is important to understand the trends of the past, and this includes having an historical look at where the employee members traditionally utilize the benefit plan.

This prior usage is a significant factor for creating new rates. Now the remaining employees on the plan have graduated to a more expensive program without any new benefits to show for the extra expense. Whether they participated in the usage or not, their rates have increased to cover off all those no longer even on the plan.

First things first—you are not alone. This is the current story for most Alberta business owners just now. But as the economy levels off and the glut of the excess usage has been paid for, normalcy of the premiums will return. Opportunity is knocking. Now is the time for a thorough review of the renewal documents to look for patterns and prepare by either carving benefits back or looking a more creative plan design options, such as administrative services only (ASO) or health spending accounts (HSA) to keep expense levels where they need to be—providing the essentials, while carving back the fat.

WAIVING OFF COVERAGE

What Can an Employee Waive?

"The employee doesn't want to be part of the benefit plan. He or she has coverage elsewhere."

Can employees waive off benefits when they have alternate coverage? Yes, but not all coverage.

On a typical benefit plan, employees must be enrolled for the life, AD&D, dependent life (if they have dependents) and short- and long-term disability (as applicable).

Employees can waive the pharmacy, health, vision and dental care only when they have spousal coverage elsewhere. Employees' spouses are not coverage for life or disability under the benefit plan. These are income-related benefits, and employers do not pay non-employee spouses a wage.

Allowing an employee to completely decline all benefit coverage has serious ramifications for the employee, his or her family and, ultimately, the company for which he or she is employed.

Let's use an example of an employee who has declined full coverage assuming that he or she was completely covered under a spouse. Now that spouse has lost coverage for one reason or another, and the employee wants to be on this benefit plan. The insurance carrier will not allow this without all family members completing an evidence of insurability questionnaire. The insured underwriter reserves the right to decline coverage. If all members of the family are approved for coverage, some of the benefits approved will still have first-year limitations.

Let's take this same scenario one step further and assume the same employee who declined this coverage incurs a disability. What now? This employee has no ability to replace his or her wage as he or she assumed he or she was covered under his or her spouse's plan (which he or she cannot be). The employee will not approach his or her spouse's employer for this coverage; however, the employee will approach his or her own employer and request to now be on the plan.

As the employee was not listed for coverage under the plan—no premiums were paid—he or she does not exist for the insurance carrier. The employer has now assumed the role of the insurer, as well as risk and liability for any and all claims arising as a result of this employee's death or disability.

Providing benefits to an employee group demands 100 percent participation from all of your employees.

CONTRACT EMPLOYEES

Providing Coverage for Different Classes

Types of Contract Employees

- Temporary employee
- People hired for a particular project, etc.

As employees, it is expected any income earned will be T-4 and that the employer will pay appropriate payroll taxes, WCB, UIC, etc. It then becomes an employer's decision as to if they wish to extend benefits to these people and an underwriting and risk issue for the insurer.

Self-Employed or Independent Contractors

These employees do not receive T-4 for income earned, and the employer does not withhold payroll taxes. Providing coverage under the employer's benefit plan for these individuals can jeopardize the individual's status as self-employed.

Canada Customs and Revenue Agency (CCRA) is of the opinion that an individual cannot be self-employed or incorporated for tax purposes and also consider themselves employees solely for eligibility on a benefit plan. In fact, CCRA are always looking for true employment relationships, and the fact that these individuals are covered under an employer-sponsored plan is viewed as strong support for the fact they are employees and not self-employed.

Section 6 (1) of the Income Tax Act exempts certain benefits that are received from the employer in the course of employment. If there is no employer-employee relationship, this section does not apply, and hence, premiums would be taxable and perhaps even the benefits from the plan.

Incorporated Employees and Consultants

The tax issues are very similar to the self-employed but not exactly the same if the individual has set up a corporation. Canada Customs and Revenue Agency has established rules to prevent true employment income from being paid to a corporation. These personal service rules will deny any corporate tax rates advantage where it would be reasonable to regard the individual, but for the existence of his own company, to be an employee of the business paying for his services. If the individual is part of the paying company's employee benefit plan, then there is a significant risk of running afoul of these personal services business rules and thus jeopardizing the tax planning that has been done. Besides this, any benefits payable from the plan may be taxable to the individual.

THE COST OF EMPLOYEE TURNOVER

What does it cost to replace employees?

One of the most critical components of success for the business owner, regardless of size, is the ability to keep the cost of doing business at a minimum. However, what many businesspeople fail to realize is that employee turnover can represent a very substantial cost and lead to erosion of the bottom line.

When an employee leaves, it will cost at least 150 percent of that person's base salary to replace him or her.

Let's say you have an employee with an annual salary of $50,000 who leaves a company. It will cost a company a minimum of $75,000 to replace that person. This cost includes the savings realized because the person has left! And all of that cost is taken away from the bottom line. We have developed a turnover cost projection model that identifies and calculates all the costs incurred.

The model indicates that the business costs and impact of employee turnover can be grouped into four major categories: 1) costs due to a person leaving; 2) hiring; 3) training; and 4) lost productivity. For purposes of illustration, I'm going to use an example of a financial analyst in a midsized company. This person is paid an annual base salary of $52,000, which works out to an hourly rate of $25, assuming a 40-hour work week.

Costs Due to a Person Leaving

When this financial analyst announces that he is leaving (to avoid awkwardness, allow me to use the pronoun *he*), he has immediately begun to transition out of the company. Even though he has given you two or three weeks' notice, his mind and full attention are not on this business anymore; this is simply human nature.

At this point, costs include the following: employees who must fill in for the person who leaves before a replacement is found; the lost productivity of the employee while he is still in his position but not fully concentrating on his job; the cost of a manager or other executive having an exit interview with the employee to determine what work remains, how to do the work, why he is leaving, etc.; the cost of training the company has provided this departing employee; the cost of lost knowledge, skills and contacts of the departing employee; the increased cost of unemployment insurance; and the possible cost of lost customers the departing employee is taking with him (or that leave because service is negatively impacted). The total of these costs can be as much as 85 percent of this position's base salary, or $45,000.

Hiring Costs

Unless there is someone to promote or the perfect person just happens to come along at the right time, there will be some costs associated with identifying and hiring a replacement for the position. These costs will include items like advertising, an employment agency, employee referral award, Internet posting and other forms of announcing the availability of the position. More money may well have to be offered to attract the right candidates. At the next stage, interviews conducted by management or hiring department staff will cost money in terms of the time they spend arranging for interviews, conducting the interviews, calling references, having discussions about the people they met and notifying candidates who did not get the job.

The time spent on these activities will also cost money in terms of lost productivity, because, with rare exceptions, these people are not employed to be full-time interviewers. The sum total of these costs will be from 15 percent of this position's base salary or approximately $8,000. This will increase to about 38 percent of the position's base salary or $20,000 if an employment agency is used.

Training Costs

Now that the person is hired for the position, she can't be expected to know absolutely everything on the first day. Costs for training include employee orientation packages, specific training to do the job and the day-to-day duties to get the job done. Even though this may be informal or on-the-job training, the time it takes for various people to impart this knowledge is costing money—especially since people who are knowledgeable enough to train others are probably also highly valuable to the company. Set the sum total of these costs at approximately 13 percent of the position's base salary or $7,000.

Lost Productivity Costs

Because this person does not come fully trained, it will take time before he is fully productive. This is true even if when promoting from within. The following formula can be used: the employee is only 25 percent productive for the first four weeks; 50 percent productive for weeks five through eight; and 75 percent productive for weeks nine through twelve. The employee will finally reach full productivity after week twelve. Since this person is being paid at the full rate of pay during this period, there are still more lost productivity costs.

During this time of lost productivity, the person's supervisor is also spending more time instructing, reviewing work and possibly correcting mistakes. (There will be some mistakes that are not caught right away and will cost money to correct down the line, such as with a customer who receives an incorrect price, invoice or actual shipment due to the new person's error.) Put the sum total of these costs at approximately 32 percent of the position's base salary or $17,000.

Adding the subtotals gives a total of approximately $77,000 if an employment agency is not used. This figure is just about 150 percent of the original $52,000 base salary. (And remember the additional costs of employee benefits and company-paid taxes on top of that, which can range from 20 percent to 30 percent.)

The Employee as Resource, Rather Than Expenditure

For a company with $5 million in revenue and $250,000 in net income, they have just spent between $75,000 and $90,000 of that profit to replace someone! You may say that these are just "the costs of doing business," and to a certain extent, that's true. However, would you rather spend $75,000 on purchasing a new piece of equipment or use it just to maintain the status quo?

The cost of time and lost productivity is no less important or real than the costs associated with paying cash to vendors for services. This is something often overlooked or underestimated; yet in today's job market, with companies competing for skilled workers, this is becoming more and more significant.

This is not to say that all employee turnover can or should be eliminated. But given the high costs involved and the impact on productivity and customer service, a well-thought-out program designed to retain employees can easily pay for itself in a very short period of time. For all of these many reasons, it is a good idea to start taking a hard look at your benefits, your policies and the intangibles that make your company a desirable place to work.

COORDINATION OF BENEFITS

Utilizing the Spousal Plan

Rising costs concern everyone. Plan members who utilize coordination of benefits (COB) can recoup up to 100 percent of eligible health and dental expenses.

In all cases where benefits are being coordinated, the insurer will apply any deductibles, maximums or coverage limitations in accordance with the policy before payments are issued.

COB is when a plan member with family coverage has a spouse with family coverage under his or her benefit plan as well. Industry-wide guidelines developed by the Canadian Life and Health Insurance Association (CLHIA) establish a consistent handling process for all insurance companies to follow when processing health and dental claims.

Consistent Handling Process

The long and short of the coverage rules are, if the claim is for the plan member, the claim is submitted first through his or her plan and second through the spouse's plan. The opposite is true for the spouse—a claim would be submitted first through the spouse's plan and second through the plan member's benefits. When both parents have benefits, the CLHIA guidelines suggest claims for eligible dependents flow through the parent whose date of birth falls earlier in the calendar year.

In most cases, even in the event of a divorce or separation, the same dependent child rules apply.

If your spouse's insurance plan happens to be with the same carrier, perhaps even the same company, the same rules apply. The employee and spouse must refer to each other's policy number when submitting claims, so the insurance carrier can coordinate benefits available for each plan automatically.

When COB is utilized, you make the most of coverage available through your benefit plan.

CONTINUATION OF COVERAGE

Terminations, Reinstatements Periods, Leaves of Absence

There is often confusion around this particular topic, especially as rules do change within the industry and how each carrier addresses these changes is specific to them and the policy contract each employer holds.

There are some universals, such as terminations. On the date an employee is no longer active, he or she is considered terminated from the benefit plan.

If the termination date was missed, the longest the insurance carrier will backdate a termination is 60 days. For anything longer, the company is responsible to pay these premiums.

If an employee terminates and is rehired, he or she can be reinstated on the benefit plan with no waiting period applied within three months from the effective date of their termination. (This timeline can vary by contract.) If the employee is away longer than three months and is rehired, then the employee is required to complete a new enrollment form, serve the waiting period and be treated as a new hire. Please note that the employer always has the right to waive the waiting period so the employee becomes effective on his or her date of rehire.

If an employee is temporarily laid off or on a leave of absence, insurance may be continued for the following maximum periods, provided the premium continues to be paid. (Note that this may vary per contract.)

- Life insurance can be continued up to six months from the date of termination
- Long-term disability may be continued for up to one month from the date of termination. There is no continuation of the disability benefit due to layoff.
- Short-term disability may be continued up to one month from the date of termination.
- All other benefits may be continued for up to six months from the date of termination.

Maternity and paternity leaves are restricted by existing provincial government guidelines; however, in general, the employer has three choices:

- Continue all coverage for duration of leave (premiums must continue to be paid).
- Continue all benefit coverage except disability (premiums must continue to be paid).
- Extend no coverage.

In all cases, the employer's actions must be consistent in applying the same decisions equally to all employees within the same classification as described in the benefit details of the contract.

BEWARE TOO EASY

Taking Care of the Pocketbook

Anyone who knows me more than ten minutes knows how much I love going to the coffee shop to meet with clients and friends. The atmosphere suits me, and despite never being advertised as such, there is little to no cell phone use, so we truly chat without interference.

It will come as no surprise then that I use a preloaded coffee card for paying at the till. It is simple and convenient. But it is not an auto reloadable card, and here's why:

A little while ago, a young-ish employee had his wallet stolen. He acted promptly and had all of his credit and debit cards replaced, but he forgot all about the coffee card his parents purchased for him while he was at university. This was a reloadable coffee card on an automatic monthly withdrawal from the folks' bank account direct onto this card.

You know where this is going. Months later, he's at the coffee shop and suddenly remembers he had a prepaid card for that franchise in the wallet that was stolen. He called his folks to see if they still supported that card. Yes, of course they did. He logged online to access the card's information.

The warning here is how easy it was to forget he even had this card. His parents never questioned the debit from their account because they had preapproved it as a gift for their son, so it was an expected transaction, a forgotten expense, month after month.

Despite their popularity, the issuers of these cards are not currently required to offer consumers free access to account information, fee disclosures and protection from loss and unauthorized transactions. In 2014, more than $220 billion was charged in the United States to prepaid cards—4 percent of all payment card purchases. Credit cards amounted to 54 percent and debit 42 percent.

This employee and his parents can only guess how much was used on that card before they stopped the auto-load. According to the franchise website, the card can carry of balance of up to $2,000 before the auto-load is disrupted.

I personally don't feel the need for an auto reload since I can easily load the card at the counter when I need to.

As criminals look for increasingly sneaky ways to grab data and get their hands on anything with value, loyalty cards and gift cards are in danger of becoming the latest proxy in the ongoing war. Criminals are learning how to turn rewards programs, points and prepaid cards into cash.

The question you ultimately need to ask yourself is this: Are all my personal details, e-mails, addresses and credit card numbers worth the bit of extra time it will take to reload the card right at the counter? As easy and convenient as it is to use the card, it's just as easy to lose your identity and hard-earned money.

THE PERKS OF BENEFITS

Wrap It up with a Bow

Group benefits are the best gift to give employees.

While every dollar an employer pays in salary is considered taxable, every dollar an employer contributes toward health and dental premiums is non-taxable (outside the province of Quebec). That's the gift that can save employees anywhere from 26 to 44 percent on expenses in incurred tax depending on the individual tax bracket. How nice is that!

Although any life and disability premiums paid by an employer are reported on the T4 slip as taxable, there are some other perks companies can offer to staff that the tax man won't be able to bite into.

An employer is allowed to give gifts and awards worth up to $500 a year without tax. Christmas parties are also tax deductible as long as they cost less than $100 per person

How about those frequent flyer points? Yes, job-related flying charges on a personal credit card to collect frequent flyer or reward points are not considered a taxable benefit, even if reimbursed, so long as they are not converted to cash.

The nontaxable value of an education is lost when the employer pays tuition for a course not benefiting the company. If, however, the course is considered to develop or upgrade skills an employee needs to do his or her job or take on future assignments, then the money is tax free.

If an employee moved due to a transfer, the expenses related to that move can be reimbursed by the employer without attracting a tax hit. Those expenses can include

- moving costs and storage expenses;
- vehicle expenses, meals and accommodation associated with moving you and members of your household to your new residence;
- real estate commissions and legal fees to purchase the new residence when the old residence has been sold;
- mortgage prepayment and lease cancellation fees; and
- costs of disconnecting and reconnecting utilities.

Keeping ahead of the curve means home computers used for work are non-taxable benefits as long as home computers are made available to all employees.

Wearing the logo, such as on T-shirts and other swag, including mugs, pens and trophies, is not taxable.

In all things, consider what you had to earn this Christmas season to pay for gifts, parties and other luxuries. Receiving those items tax free would have meant much greater savings.

PLUS TAX

Financial Literacy

My poor son.

In an effort to teach financial literacy to my nine-year-old, I had him go through the process of setting up his own account.

Yes, we had set an account up for each of our children when they were born; however, going through the experience of setting up your account and feeling the responsibility of that account is what we wanted to achieve with this exercise, so we scheduled a meeting at the bank.

On the day of the appointment, my son took his identification—SIN and health-care card—walked into the branch and asked to speak to the person with whom we had scheduled the get-together. He listened carefully, if not excitedly, to her go through the parameters of the account and how important it was to always set aside a certain amount of income (as received at birthdays and special occasions) to pure savings before handing him his debit card.

With these formalities out of the way, money in the bank and so much set aside for savings, he was eager to try out his new debit card, so off we went to the store. A Skylander figurine was the only item on his list. He looked at the price and pulled out the teller slip, which showed his balance on his account. He said happily, "I can get this one."

It was a bubble buster better heard from me than to have the embarrassing encounter of disappointment when he found out the same thing at the till: "Plus tax."

In the longwinded, over-the-head explanation of tax that my son essentially forgot as soon as he adjusted his purchasing capacity to a

Skylander he could afford, I walked away exhausted and glad I only had to explain GST and not an additional provincial sales tax!

The bottom line is this: it's no fun to pay tax. Fortunately, when properly designed, life, AD&D, dependent life, short- and long-term disability and critical illnesses are designed on an employee group benefit plan to pay out tax free upon claim. Even better, pharmacy, health, dental and vision care are all nontaxable benefits in Canada, outside the province of Quebec.

DISTRACTED

Keeping the Focus

Talk of the distracted driver makes me think about all of the things consumers get distracted about.

Drive down any metro road at any given time, and see the many distractions—other drivers, mosquitoes that have snuck into the vehicle, the radio talk show host's opinion, my kids and more. But road signs have reached a whole new level of distraction. Never mind the old-fashioned wooden advertising; we're now in the electronic age, and these new signs—jumbo billboard types that used to be a rarity to see at a concert in a stadium—are now the norm on the side of the road, not just to advertise but also entertain as you drive by or sit in traffic. Never mind trying to figure out your next turn or even what street you're on. These new signs deliver what to eat, what to wear, where to go to do these things and how long it will take to get there. Who needs GPS?

Of course, the idea of the new law is to have your eyes on the road, but the message—so glittery and available—is taking us off course, straying us from the intended purpose.

Isn't this a metaphor for most things in life and business?

With the intention of getting things done, we are often waylaid by the multitude of distractions, the glitter and the want. The want often makes us forgo the need, so instead of having the right benefit plan, which covers the needs and takes care of the things we want, we get distracted by the glitz, the show, the sale.

Employers, because they worry the employees will balk, will forgo the protection of the employees' salary—the disability—in favor of items like vision care coverage. Will that employee care about a couple hundred dollars in optical when he or she can no longer work and now has no income coming in to support his or her family and daily needs? Unlikely. If you had a cash machine that provided you with money as you need it, would you insure it? For sure. That is your employees. They are the cash machine for their family, and if they have not insured their ability to earn against the multitude of harm that can come their way, nothing else on the benefit plan will matter. At the point, there is no income.

In the business of employee benefits, brokers are jaded. We know people need coverage for life and disability insurance, health and dental coverage, but our clients get distracted (scared away) by the cost of implications and swayed by glittery mixed messaging.

The point of the commentary is to stay focused. Keep your eyes on the road and job at hand at providing benefits to cover the necessities. Engage qualified, competent consultants who will ensure you understand exactly what you are buying and why you are buying. If you don't have a need for it, don't buy it; it really is that simple. That way when the time comes, you have the benefit coverage necessary at an acceptable price point without any barriers to successful outcomes.

The Promise to the Employees

When an employer hires an employee, they enter a contractual obligation. Yes, a wage will be provided for duties as outlined being completed. In that, taxes must be filed and registration and paperwork must be adhered to. The contract is the promise by each party to participate, and only through active participation from both sides will the contract obligations be fulfilled.

By the same token, when a company enters into a benefit arrangement with a provider, there are contracts completed with each side agreeing to participate. The employer agrees to pay premiums, and the provider agrees to pay claims as they arise.

In this same contract is the understanding all active, eligible employees will participate.

In implementing such a plan, the employer therefore makes a promise to their biggest asset—their employees—to invest in the well-being, the stability of these workers, to ensure their investment into their company will be successful.

A benefit plan can comprise many different elements from life insurance and disability to health, dental, wellness and flex accounts. What matters, though, is the promise of participation from all parties to ensure coverage is there when it is needed.

Catastrophic—for those unforeseen circumstances resulting in a risk of loss of life, risk of loss of income and risk of a catastrophic event. These elements are pooled to ensure the risk is spread among the masses.

Bricks of coverage—for those day-to-day needs of health, professional paramedical services and basic dental claims.

The mortar—providing choice of coverage for employees. These flexible health spending accounts fill in the gaps of coverage between existing benefits and spousal coverage to top up coverage where it is needed most. This may be for items such as orthodontics, vision care and holistic remedies.

As in all things benefit, first consider what promise you want to make to the employees regarding their coverage—what is the goal?—and then set to work creating a plan. A well-thought-out, well-designed benefit plan will always be seen as a strategic element to the overall business platform of the company, creating long-term success and fulfilling the promise.

REPORTING SALARIES

What Benefits Are Salary Based?

Life and disability benefits are based upon an employee's income. To ensure the coverage level is correct, please feel free to use the following guideline when reporting salaries for each insured person.

For Employees

Where an employee receives a T4 or T4A from the company, income for group insurance purposes would be the same as the T4 or T4A income. This amount reflects all amounts paid to the employee, including salary, fees, bonuses and taxable benefits.

For Owners, Shareholders and Key Employees of Incorporated Firms

For these individuals, the insurable income would include all T4 or T4A income as well as T5 amounts:

- Annual salary and commissions $ _____
- Management fees $ _____
- Bonuses $ _____
- Company dividends (two years average T5) $ _____

    Total $ _____

For Commissioned Individuals or Owners of Unincorporated Proprietorships and Partnerships

For these individuals, the insurable income would be based on the "net income" shown under self-employed income on the T1 general return as illustrated below. Take the current- and prior-year amounts, and base the amount of coverage on the average of the two.

Self-Employed Income

Business income	Gross 162	$38,000.00	Net 135	$28,500
Professional income	Gross 164	$_____	Net 137	$_____
Commission income	Gross 166	$_____	Net 139	$_____
Farming income	Gross 168	$_____	Net 141	$_____
Fishing income	Gross 170	$_____	Net 143	$_____

- Net income (current year) $_____
- Net income (prior year) $_____
  Average of last two years $_____

Please note: At the time of a disability claim, individuals may be required to confirm their income by providing copies of their current T1, T4 or T5 income tax forms.

EMPLOYEE TERMINATIONS

Benefit Coverage and Severance

The decline of the Alberta economy has seen more requests for extending benefits due to the severance period for layoff (termination).

Companies who have implemented employment contracts and corporate policies already have a plan in place for these contingencies. However, for those that don't, consult with an employment lawyer.

The following are some generalities and are by no means to be considered legal advice.

When active employees are terminated, it is important the correct termination date is applied. Note, an employee's benefit coverage ends when employment terminates, which for an employee actively at work is typically the last day worked.

Severance or termination pay is the reference used for salary paid in lieu of notice for the statutory notice period. This pay may also include vacation, salary or overtime owed to the employee at the time of termination.

In the province of Alberta, even when termination pay is received, the employee's benefits still end on the last day worked.

A severance agreement differs from employment contracts. Once the employee-employer relationship ends, the insured no longer meets the definition of an insurable employee and is no longer eligible for coverage under the group insurance contract.

There may be situations where the employer wishes to extend benefits beyond the date of termination as part of the severance agreement. Under certain circumstances, depending on the insured carrier or provider, they may consider extending coverage for basic life and AD&D

(typically to a maximum of $250,000) dependent life insurance, health and dental care benefits for a limited time, and the extension applies to all employees in a similar circumstance.

Due to the policy wording of having to be "actively at work," some benefits, such as short- and long-term disability, cannot be extended.

If an employer is considering extending benefits into a severance period, it is important that they contact both an employment lawyer and the insurance provider prior to offering this to the employee to determine which benefits can be extended, to what amount and for how long, as well as establishing the costs involved.

Again, this information is intended for informational purposes only and is not intended as legal or tax advice. Always contact a lawyer or accountant for specific tax and legal counseling.

Jurisdiction	Length of service	Statutory Notice Period
Alberta	More than three months, less than two years	One week
	Two years, but less than four years	Two weeks
	Four years, but less than six years	Four weeks
	Six years, but less than eight years	Five weeks
	Eight years, but less than ten years	Six weeks
	Ten years or more	Eight weeks

THE COSTS OF SENIORS

The Aging Workforce

The headlines reads, "Canada to See a 40 Percent Increase in Cancer Patients."

This *Globe and Mail* article goes on to report that this staggering statistic is due to the "rising tide of seniors." In fact, way down the page, the article reveals the incident rates for cancer have held steady; death rates are down, and survival rates are up.

Wait—what?

The real story, it seems, is that the boomers, who still amass the largest segment of the population, are getting up there, and as they age, researchers predict, they will flood the system with their needs.

What we need to do is this: invest, invest, invest in long-term planning and prevention.

- Quit smoking.
- Lose weight.
- Stay out of the sun.
- Have regular health screenings.

There's nothing new there. It's common sense, really. However, that advice is easier said than done.

At the heart of this is planning. As Canadians, we used to think it was only those in the United States who had to worry about the cost of health care in retirement. This was never really true; however, with so many facing a future where the social safety net is rather thin, chatter of this kind is big news.

The need for health care is never more prevalent than in the retirement years, yet this is a time when availability of "protection" for these services is severely lacking. Sure, the basics are covered—generic drugs, hospital care and routine doctor visits. But what about professional doctors, such as physiotherapy, chiropractic and audiology? Vision care? Dental services?

How many retirement plans include covering these extra costs?

It's one of those things where thinking ahead now can save a lot of stress later. Be sure to include this line item in any long-term financial plan.

Section 5

Employee Death Benefits
Replacement of Salary

THE REAL WORLD

A Glimpse of Real Life

A midsized company offers a benefit plan that includes life insurance equal to double the annual salary, accidental death and dismemberment, dependent life insurance for those employees with dependents, short- and long-term disability benefits, plus a generous health, dental and vision care plan, which includes a point-of-sale drug card. To top the benefits, the company also offers a matching group RRSP.

The benefit plan has been set up as a mandatory benefit plan, meaning all employees must participate in the life and disability coverage, with the ability to "waive" off coverage for the health and dental portion of the plan if the employee has coverage through another plan via his or her spouse.

It sounds great on paper, but in reality, there are always those employees who feel they are invincible and have no need for the insurance, and despite the best efforts of plan administrators, they will not enroll in the plan until something happens, and make no mistake: it always does.

Bring on the black cape; it's grim reaper time. But if you only knew just how often this same scenario plays out, you would never allow an employee to opt off the plan.

True events played out hundreds of times. There's a great plan. Then one employee has health and dental through the spouse. Despite being told the spousal plan does not cover the employee for life or disability coverage, the employee refuses benefits. Over and over the employee argues he or she has no need for insurance. The employer never completes the forms. As far as the insurer is concerned, the employee doesn't exist because the enrollment is never submitted or received.

Now this employee is invincible!

Until they are not. More true stories.

Maybe it's a year or two, or maybe it's as soon as three months later, but this same employee (the invincible one) suffers a stroke, or he gets into a car wreck, or maybe he was the fellow working on the farm who broke his back, or was it the time he was working on the old truck and the hydraulics let loose and crushed his arm?

Regardless of the endless scenarios, it does happen: accident, injury, illness—it is disability.

Once treatment is received and life suddenly becomes as clear as a winter breeze, the first phone call goes to the employer to confirm the benefit plan has disability coverage.

"Yeah, I know I turned it down before, but now I need it, and hey, I'm willing to pay the premiums if I have to. It's pretty tight just now with no income coming in, and all of my existing insurance is tied to my house, car and other loans. I didn't realize that before. I thought I had coverage, but I've just gone through everything, and I don't." Then the employee continues in his or her own terms. "When I was offered the plan, I forgot I have a family that needs to eat and be clothed, and bills have to be paid. None of that is covered under my spouse's plan."

Remember, insurance carriers have no emotions. If we have lived through this scenario hundreds of times, just how many thousand songs do you think the insurance carriers have listened to? Just like with car insurance, you cannot be covered when you are sitting in the middle of the intersection in an accident. So too does the same logic apply when something happens to the employee. As hard-hearted as it may sound, there is no coverage available when the wreck has already occurred.

Judgment

By all accounts, she wasn't a well-liked employee—even after her death. Her husband even less so.

She died by suicide.

The owner and adviser at the time determined no life insurance would be payable. No claim was submitted—done.

Not so fast.

Employee benefit plans have no suicide clause as individual policies have. Even individual policies only stipulate (for the most part) a two-year caveat for death due to suicide. Not only was her beneficiary entitled to life insurance, but the plan also included a 24-month survivor benefit for the health and dental portion of the plan.

Insurance doesn't have a personality. Insurance doesn't care whether a person was liked at the office. The insurance carrier pays claims because a premium was paid for certain coverage. This woman had worked at this company for many years and paid her premium via a payroll deduction all of those years. For that reason, her beneficiary was entitled to the insurance money and the benefits provided under the health and dental portion of the plan.

Though this grievous error was not caught until more than 14 months after the woman died, the insurance provider paid the claim in accordance to the policy and upheld the survivor benefits as well.

When in doubt, don't assume; ask.

DYING

When There Is No Other Insurance in Place

"It's my first time dying. I'm just trying to get used to it," she said in a forced, flippant voice as we got to the heart of why she was calling.

Her words faltered, and she coughed.

This is certainly not the type of call I ever expected to take.

You see, when the call began, she was questioning her coverage, as many employees do. The majority of calls are from employees asking about and confirming their coverage. They have read their benefit booklet (or not) and have clarification questions and require explanation. But this was different, obviously.

Inoperable, her doctors had pronounced her terminal, with anywhere from three weeks to three months to live. She was doing her best in the time she had left, she said, to get her affairs in order. In her words, that's all she'd been doing since receiving the tragic news.

This instance struck me and continues to trouble e.

For this woman, her final days were spent planning and preparing. She was using her limited and waning energy to ensure there was enough for the kids, her husband—protection for those left behind. Other than the group life policy, there was no other individual coverage. There was the insurance on the mortgage, which would pay her portion of the mortgage, but what about all of the other expenses? Funeral, taxes, other—what about the lack of a will? What about probate?

Some will shrug and say, "Not my issue. I'm gone. I don't want anyone getting rich off my death." Getting rich off of someone's death is not even part of the equation. Insurance is so those left don't carry a financial loss in addition to the loss of a beloved family member. How about burial with dignity.

And this was her train of thought as she was talking to me. She opened up to likely the only person who got it and understood her burning need to leave without causing a burden.

If it wasn't important, she wouldn't have called. If it didn't mean anything, she would have shrugged as well and said, "Well, I'll leave it to them to deal with." But she didn't think that way when she knew the end was near. As her final days came to a close, her number-one concern was to ensure those left behind would be taken care of the way that she would have taken care of them had she been there to provide it herself.

The sad part, as I see it, is that she used her final time having to worry about these things instead of just being with the family who loved her dearly.

My message: Don't go out with regrets. Take the time now, and meet with someone who can put everything in place so when you are not there, everything carries on as you would have wished it to.

TO BE HUMAN

Life Insurance on a Group Benefit Plan

Death is tragic.

When the bereaved have to take care of the deceased's final expenses—funeral costs, debts, taxes—death becomes cruel.

Among other reason, people purchase insurance to soften or eliminate the financial burden for those left behind.

However, there are many types of life insurance, and knowing what you have purchased can make all of the difference to those grieving.

An individual policy, whether term, whole life or universal life, is owned by the individual purchasing the policy.

A group life insurance benefit, whether a percentage of salary or a flat benefit amount, is owned by the company (employer) offering this benefit to his or her employees.

A group benefit plan has many advantages, not least of which is the ability to offer insured coverage to those individuals who would otherwise not be able to obtain an individual policy due to health or lifestyle circumstances.

But again, it is vital to know what you have.

Recently we addressed a death of an individual whose only coverage was provided by the group insurance plan. The individual named three beneficiaries for the proceeds: her spouse and two children, one dependent and one not.

All of this may seem straightforward on the surface, but it was not.

- The will disputed the beneficiaries.
- No trustee form was completed for the minor.
- All three beneficiaries had to complete the life claim form, which slowed the process, leaving room for errors in its completion.

In the end, the will had no bearing over the life proceeds as the will would only supersede life insurance "owned" by the deceased. The group policy was "owned" by the corporation. Because of a lack of trustee appointment, the spouse had to obtain a legal declaration affirming parentage, redo the life claim report and provide a copy of the minor's birth certificate.

Now, in addition to suffering the loss of a loved one, bills and administrative and financial issues are heaped onto the bereaved.

Death will never be easy, and it never should be, but the cruelty of paperwork can certainly be lessened.

Don't discount the value of the group life benefit and neglect the simple paperwork associated with getting it right the first time.

THE HERO OR THE HEEL?

Life Insurance—Never Enough

Sometimes the hero and sometimes the heel—it depends on the perspective.

Given the many options and factors associated with building a benefit plan, employers do their very best to accommodate their employees' wishes (the needs with the wants) when placing a plan. Like a blueprint for building a house, the strategy behind benefits forms the foundation for both the compensation strategy as well as the business outlook for the future of its largest investment—the employees.

As benefit brokers, we have jaded personalities; we are the salesman, but we are also the people educated on the products. When a broker sits in front of a potential client running through the various benefits available, we know that disability insurance is important. We know that for most Canadian employees, the group disability benefit is the only protection these employees have in place in the event of a disabling event, be that illness, disease or accident. We also know beyond a shadow of doubt, because we are first and foremost human, that no one wants to pay for the benefit. But there is a need for it!

All of this goes through an employer's mind as they are deciding which benefits to put in place, how much of each benefit and how they are going to approach their employees with their portion of the costs.

Sometimes to accommodate all of the different opinions and mixed messaging, employers will allocate classification of their workforce. There may be a class of employees with one set of benefits, depending on their length of service, their job duties, etc., whatever commonality ties these workers together as a subset of the overall group. It is then the employer's responsibility to let the insurance carrier know when an employee no longer meets the requirements of that particular sub group and needs to be moved into another class. Insurers cannot be expected to make that decision. They need to be told when to move that employee, make salary changes and terminations, etc.

Then there is another issue—say that an employee should have been moved into another class, but the benefits were enhanced in the other class and therefore the employee would pay more in that classification and opts to remain in the existing class, paying less for less benefit. There is more take-home pay in the employee's mind. Only the employer and the employee know this. There is no paper record, no one at the carrier office has been notified and there are no records. No one outside of the two of them can really know the reasons.

Yet the employer is now off side on so many levels.

Add to this, the employee dies. The employee had been sick for a long time prior to dying. The spouse, having gone through what can only be imagined, is older, has no income of her own and has now lost not only the spouse but also her sole source of income.

There are no heroes in this true tale. The employee opted to remain in the plan at a reduced benefit level to save three to five dollars a month, only to deny the surviving spouse tens of thousands of dollars that could have made the difference of her remaining in their family home, being able to make ends meet, and surviving her remaining years in small comfort—not luxury, small comfort.

She probably never even knew he had the choice.

TO BE HUMAN

Life Insurance on a Group Benefit Plan

Death is tragic.

When the bereaved have to take care of the deceased final expenses: funeral costs, debts, taxes—death becomes cruel.

Among other reasons, people purchase insurance to soften or eliminate the financial burden for those left behind.

However, there are many types of life insurance, and knowing what you have purchased can make all of the difference to those grieving.

An individual policy, whether term, whole life or universal life, is owned by the individual purchasing the policy.

A group life insurance benefit, whether a percentage of salary or a flat benefit amount, is owned by the company (employer) offering this benefit to employees.

A group benefit plan has many advantages, not least of which is the ability to offer insured coverage to those individuals who would otherwise not be able to obtain an individual policy due to health or lifestyle circumstances.

But again, it is vital to know what you have.

Recently we addressed a death of an individual whose only coverage was provided by the group insurance plan. The individual named three beneficiaries for the proceeds: her spouse and two children, one dependent and one not.

All of this may seem straightforward on the surface, but it was not.

- The will disputed the beneficiaries.
- No trustee form was completed for the minor.
- All three beneficiaries had to complete the life claim form, which slowed the process, leaving room for errors in its completion.

In the end, the will had no bearing over the life proceeds as the will would only supersede life insurance owned by the deceased. The group policy was "owned" by the corporation. Because of a lack of trustee appointment, the spouse had to obtain a legal declaration affirming parentage, redo the life claim report and provide a copy of the minor's birth certificate.

Now, in addition to suffering the loss of a loved one, bills, administrative and financial issues are heaped onto the bereaved.

Death will never be easy, and it never should be, but the cruelty of paperwork can certainly be lessened.

Don't discount the value of the group life benefit and neglect the simple paperwork associated with getting it right the first time.

GENETIC TESTING

Bill S-201

With the ability to reveal an individual's risk of developing various illnesses and disease, genetic testing is expected to transform the practice of medicine. However, those with known family history of certain conditions may opt not to take such tests for fear of results disclosure and the subsequent discrimination. The impact of such choices is far reaching when it comes to a person's lifestyle and access to medical care.

In the insurance industry, there is a growing concern that asking for this type of information will prevent people from seeking or obtaining needed insured protection. This and other considerations has led to the introduction of the private member's bill (Bill S-201). If enacted, this legislation would prevent insurers (and others) from either requiring genetic testing or requesting the results. In turn, this may have an impact on pricing for insured products and their availability.

Bill S-201 (the bill) would prohibit insurance companies from requiring an individual to undergo a genetic test (as defined as a test that analyzes DNA, RNA or chromosomes for purposes such as the prediction of disease or vertical transmission risk or monitoring, diagnosis or prognosis) as a condition of purchasing an insurance policy (which includes life, living benefits and group insurance). Further, this bill would prohibit insurance companies from refusing to provide life insurance coverage because the applicant has refused to disclose the results of a genetic test. As well, an insurance company (or other persons including insurance agents) will be prohibited from collecting, using or disclosing the results of a genetic test of the individual without the individual's written consent.

From the insurer's perspective, because the fundamental basis of insurance is the concept of equal knowledge between the insured and the underwriter of the insured product, if the applicant keeps this information private and confidential, the insurance company will ultimately pay out more unexpected claims, and this will eventually increase the cost of insurance. An increase in cost may mean fewer Canadians purchase insurance for themselves.

At the present time, the insurance industry does have a code whereby they don't require an applicant to go for genetic testing, nor do they require the results from these tests taken by family members. However, because within each provincial insurance act there is a provision that any material fact relevant in an application must be disclosed, Bill S-201 is in direct conflict with provincial legislation. In January, the insurance industry announced that it will voluntarily agree not to request genetic testing for life insurance up to $250,000, which blankets close to 85 percent of all current insurance applications.

While the underlying rationale to prevent discrimination is sound, all sides must be considered. We will continue to monitor this and other legislation relevant and of concern to our clients. We always welcome your feedback.

THE VALUE OF OFFERING SHORT-TERM DISABILITY BENEFITS

Employment Insurance (EI) is a form of worker wage protection, which began in the 1930s. For reasons of unemployment due to lack of work or being disabled, the employee is entitled to 55 percent of their pay up to the set weekly limit. This payment is taxable.

The changes to the employment insurance benefit make me think of a blanket ripped in half, where the top is sewn to the bottom, now comprising the middle and calling it a new blanket.

No.

Changing the initial waiting period for coverage to begin from two weeks to one and then taking the additional week on at the end only serves to annoy and frustrate users in need of the program. When EI is used for short-term sickness benefits, these kinds of changes only serve to heighten the need for private short-term disability coverage.

When employers offer a short-term disability program under their benefit plan, they are then entitled to a savings on the EI premium.

Short-term disability benefits offer 24-hour coverage (i.e., income protection) for employees in case of an accident or sickness, on the job or off.

While many organizations count on their employees receiving disability benefits from Employment Insurance (EI) to carry them through a period of disability, there are risks. The following are some of the dangers associated with relying solely on EI:

- Business owners are not covered.
- Benefits are paid at 55 percent of the employee's gross income.
- Benefits are fully taxable.
- Benefits are capped.
- Benefits are payable after a one-week waiting period, with an additional week tacked on the end.

A short-term disability plan provides the following advantages:

- Business owners are covered.
- Benefits are paid typically paid at 67 percent of the employee's gross income or higher.
- Benefits are not taxable, as long as the employee pays the premium portion for the benefit.
- The employer decides on the overall maximum, and the amount payable is based on salary earned.
- The waiting period is at the time of inception, typically the first day in the event of an accident or hospitalization and seven days in the event of an illness.

Consider all the options for casting aside the advantages of a short-term disability program. Remember, companies can take full advantage of the Employment Insurance Premium Reduction Program by ensuring the waiting period for receiving this benefit is fewer than 15 days.

Employers should always assess the pros and cons of both programs—EI and STD—before deciding on what will be the best option for short-term wage loss replacement strategies.

BENEFICIARY DESIGNATION

Choosing a Beneficiary Is Important

Choosing a beneficiary of the proceeds payable under a life insurance policy can be one of the most important decisions to be made when developing an estate plan. For many, these proceeds form a substantial portion of the estate available for distribution to heirs.

Therefore, it is important that the estate-planning objectives of the insured be carefully considered before a beneficiary designation is made.

The legal framework for proper designation of a beneficiary has been established by the Uniform Insurance Act in each of the common law provinces and the Civil Code in Quebec. This legislation also provides guidance for resolving disputes when a designation is unclear or ambiguous. In this section we will review some of the important principles to keep in mind when advising clients on this very important aspect of purchasing a life insurance product.

How Is a Beneficiary Designation Made?

The only legal formulary required by life insurance legislation for a beneficiary designation is that it must be made in writing. It is not even required to have a witness to the signature of the person making the designation. It may be made in the contract of insurance or contained in an entirely separate document. Although the beneficiary designation is most often found in the contract of insurance, it is not unusual to see it included in a will. In fact, the Uniform Act and Civil Code contain specific provisions respecting the validity of designations made in wills.

Can a Designation Be Revoked?

Generally, the designation of a beneficiary is revocable and may be altered at any time by the insured. It is irrevocable only if the insured so provides in the declaration. However, in Quebec, a declaration in favor of a spouse is presumed to be irrevocable unless expressly stated otherwise. Remember that an irrevocable beneficiary designation cannot be changed without the consent of the beneficiary.

Does a Designation Have to Be Filed with the Insurer?

A beneficiary designation is valid even though it is filed with the insurance company. However, if a designation has been declared irrevocable, it is not effective as such until the declaration is filed with the insurer. Failure to file an irrevocable designation does not invalidate it—the designation simply operates as an ordinary revocable beneficiary designation.

An insurance company is entitled to rely on its most recently filed beneficiary designation. An individual named in an unfiled declaration will not have a claim against the insurer if it pays the beneficiary on record without knowledge of a later unfiled declaration. Therefore, it is important that all designations be filed, and it is essential if it is an irrevocable designation.

How Should the Beneficiary Be Identified?

It is important to properly identify the beneficiary who is to receive the life insurance proceeds. It is best to refer to the person by name, although it is acceptable to describe the beneficiary by relationship to the insured or to the life insured. If there is more than one beneficiary, the share of the proceeds allocated to each should be specified in the declaration. (This may be different in Quebec.)

If the designation is not clear as to whom the insured intended to benefit, the law will assist as follows: If the description of the beneficiary is both by name and relationship and there is a conflict, the name will govern.

Designation of a spouse means a legal spouse and not a common-law spouse.

A designation in favor of children will benefit all children born to the measuring life at the time of death of the life insured, whether or not born at the date the designation was made.

Designation of "my heirs," "my assigns," or "my next of kin" will be considered a designation in favor of the estate of the insured and not a designation in favor of certain individuals.

Can Insurance Proceeds Be Left "In Trust" for Children?

In the common law provinces, insurance legislation specifically provides that an insured may appoint a trustee as a beneficiary. A designation of "X, in trust for Y" does create a trust relationship between X and Y. X will be required to hold proceeds of the policy in trust for Y. With nothing more, X will be governed by provincial trustee legislation as to how to invest and administer the trust funds and Y will be entitled to the insurance money upon reaching the age of majority.

If it is desired that the insurance money be held in trust for a longer period of time or the insured wishes to direct the manner and timing of payment of monies to the beneficiary, a trust should be created. This can be done in a separate trust agreement or in the insurer's will. Such a trust is often referred to as an insurance trust. The declaration of beneficiary should refer to "X, trustee under a trust created by (name) on ———, 2018." The declaration should clearly refer to the policy for which the trust being created should expressly revoke any previous designation and should state that it is an insurance designation under the applicable provincial legislation. If these requirements are met, the proceeds will flow directly into the trust and not into the estate of the deceased, even if the trust is created in the will.

In Quebec, a formal document should always be drafted creating the trust.

Summary

Careful consideration should be given in designating the beneficiary of a life insurance policy. The decision should both be made in isolation but in the context of the entire estate plan of the insured. Once decided, the designation should be carefully drafted to ensure that all beneficiaries are adequately described and that the division of benefits is accurately reflected of more than one beneficiary is named. If the proceeds are to be held in trust for beneficiaries, a trust document should be prepared to instruct the trustee regarding administration of the fund as well as how and when to pay monies to the beneficiaries.

PROTECTION OF INCOME

Income from Disability Claims

When I was younger, I had a conversation my creator and confirmed that when I was placed on this earth, nothing bad would happen to me.

I should have gotten that in writing!

Despite the lack of an eternal contract, I did have the ability and foresight to plan for "just in case." So what's your plan when the terms of your contract for everlasting life and no disability are broken?

Statistics for disability are staggering considering one in four will suffer a disability before retirement. Remember, a disability that lasts two years will likely extend to lifetime.

Disability insurance is an integral part of any long-term financial plan, despite your age. A disability can be more financially devastating than death. Income is the foundation of the lifestyle you created, and if that income is no longer available, what do you have to maintain the household and pay expenses—life costs?

An acquaintance recently confided that despite being covered for his unexpected disability by both WCB and his group benefit plan, financially things were touch and go for months, and he simply couldn't afford to take the time for the recovery his doctors recommended.

To that point, employee group benefit plans have maximums and nonevidence maximums and therefore are an unlikely source for full income protection as many employees do not bother to complete the medical questionnaire necessary to achieve the overall maximum, and for those higher-income earners, the monthly maximum may fall substantially short of their needs.

Those who wait to implement a benefit plan will likely miss their golden opportunity: lower rates and preferred rating potential.

No matter how young or healthy, disability does not discriminate against the old or infirm, and once a person is unable to work, well, then it's too late.

For those who think the Canada Pension Plan or some form of social government program will meet their financial needs, becoming disabled and trying to depend on that minimum income is a rude and rough awakening, if they are even approved for coverage.

When considering whether it is worth it to purchase individual disability coverage with the assumption it will never be used, consider adding a return-of-premium option. When US-based insurer Guardian reports more than $294 million paid in disability income, can you really afford not to be covered?

The Nonevidence Maximum
The Point to Which an Insurer Will Provide
Coverage Regardless of Health Concerns

A nonevidence maximum (NEM) is the amount of insurance a plan member (employee) can apply and be accepted for without needing to submit additional medical information. This means, regardless of any preexisting health conditions, that an employee would be covered up to prespecified limits of insured coverage.

Ensuring the maximum nonevidence limits for the plan members helps to attract and retain valuable employees by offering convenient plan design choices to meet their needs and provide these employees and their families with greater financial security.

Important to Note

Though the rates for the benefits do not change, the cost will increase because the volume of insurance has increased. For instance, if an employee goes from being covered for $1,000 of disability benefit to $1,500, the rate itself does not change, but the amount of insurance has changed, and therefore, the cost overall has increased.

Increasing the nonevidence maximum limit cannot be backdated on a benefit plan.

Achieving the highest NEM will also confirm any employees previously denied extra coverage due to a preexisting condition will now be covered up to the new prespecified limit.

For each group, the insurance company determines the amount of life and short- and long-term disability coverage they will offer without proof of insurability. This amount of coverage is called the nonevidence maximum and is different for each insurance company depending on the number of people being insured as a group.

If an employee is eligible for coverage beyond the nonevidence maximum, he or she must be approved for that excess coverage. Any employee who is eligible and requests coverage beyond the nonevidence maximum must provide proof of insurability. This is provided via a health questionnaire and could require a medical exam at the request of the carrier.

As an example, if an employee earned an annual salary of $45,000, the long-term disability would be broken down as follows:

$45,000/12 (months) = $3,750 per month gross salary
If the LTD is paid based upon the following formula, this is how the monthly benefit would be calculated:
73.75 percent of the first $1,250 of gross monthly salary, plus 57 percent of the next $4,083 and 53 percent of the balance
$3,750 (gross monthly salary) - $1,250=$2,500
($1,250*.7375) + ($2,500*.57)
$921.88+$1,425
$2,346.88 eligible monthly benefit

If the nonevidence maximum were capped at $1,500 per month, this employee would be eligible for an additional $846.88 per month. Unless he or she completed the medical questionnaire, he or she would not receive the full benefit if a disability were to occur.

Even if an employee were declined the additional coverage he or she applied for, the existing coverage (the nonevidence of $1,500) in place will not be impacted by these results, unless they were a late applicant to the plan.

OPEN COMMUNICATION

Be Your Own Health Care Advocate

When there is a disability, an important step in your education is to develop an open relationship with your physician or treatment provider. This can be a tough thing for some people to do initially, as you may never have had to rely on your physician for anything more than your regular physical. Some people can be intimidated by the prospect of asking their doctor a lot of questions, as they are afraid that their doctor will not want to spend the time to answer them. They may even be afraid that they will appear stupid.

Don't be afraid or intimidated! This is your life, your disability and your future! The only stupid question is the question that isn't asked. You need to develop a relationship with your physician if you are going to move beyond your disability, and if your physician doesn't have the time to spend with you to answer your questions, then you need to have an open and honest discussion about this concern that could result in a referral to another physician.

You want to know the specifics of your condition. If you can't answer the following questions, you will want to ask them of your doctor immediately:

- What are my diagnosis and prognosis and the recommended treatment regimen?
- Will there be any residual conditions from my illness or accident?
- What is my expected time for recovery?
- Will I make a full recovery?

- If not, what are the time frames so that I can expect changes or improvements?
- When can I consider a return to at least part-time or accommodated work?

Be sure to ask if a recommended treatment or therapy is covered under your health insurance so you will have an expectation of the financial consequences.

When an illness or accident results in a disabling condition, the residual effects may have long-term results that may affect your quality of life and change the way you do things. In these cases, the resulting long-term effects will have a direct impact on who you are and what you are able to do in the future. Some of the questions you will want to ask your physician at this stage are as follows:

- What are my specific restrictions and limitations, and how can they be accommodated?
- Develop a list of the activities that you perform at home and at work, and talk about each one individually. Which ones can be accommodated?
- Will these limitations be permanent?
- What are my abilities?
- When will I be able to return to work, and in what specific capacity?

Remember that any relationship takes time and open communication to develop. Your physician will get to know you better through this process, and as you gather more information, you will build confidence as well.

COMPASSION CARE

Being There When You're Needed

On January 4, 2004, employment insurance rules changed to provide up to six weeks (after the waiting period) of compassionate leave benefits for qualified applicants. The Canada Labour Code will be amended to compel employers under federal jurisdiction to grant such leaves—and preserve the jobs of employees who take them.

When introducing Bill C-28, Ottawa predicted that some 270,000 people would utilize this plan each year.

To qualify, an employee must have accumulated at least six hundred insurable hours and must provide a doctor's note certifying that the applicant has a gravely ill family member who is at significant risk of dying within six months.

Gordon McFee, the federal government's director-general of insurance policy, said the time can be taken in blocks of "a week here, a week there" within a six-month time frame. The benefit can also be shared among family members—for instance, two siblings sharing the responsibility of caring for a dying parent could each take three weeks apiece. The benefit also applies to people taking care of a dying child, a spouse or common-law partner or a spouse's parents.

Some of the logistics of the plan are summarized as follows. Payments from an employer's compassionate care leave plan will be treated the same way as benefits from a sickness, maternity or parental leave plan.

Employers are allowed to include compassionate care benefit payments in a supplementary unemployment benefit (SUB) plan, and payments from such plans will not be deducted from EI benefits payable to a claimant.

The payment of compassionate care benefits from plans that are substantially similar to SUB plans will not be treated as earnings for EI benefit purposes, which mirrors the current treatment of maternity and parental benefit payments from such plans.

Payments under a wage-loss plan related to compassionate care will not be considered earnings during the waiting period.

The exclusion that is currently permitted for maternity and parental benefits under a short-term disability plan has been extended to compassionate care benefits.

Although this Bill C-28 has a lot of merit and needs for the employee, it raises a number of issues for employers and plan sponsors regarding labor standards, administration and communication of the requirements.

Employers should consider reviewing their employee manuals and revise them as needed to reflect the introduction of compassionate care leave and any specific policies adopted regarding this leave.

While conducting this review, employers may also want to consider enacting a corporate policy regarding all leave of absence and disability as it relates to their benefit program and how long these benefits will continue in case such a situation arises.

SUB

Supplemental Unemployment Benefits

The process described below may vary depending upon the specifics of each individual case.

If you are an employer who provides your employees with a supplement to the employment insurance benefits received in cases of temporary stoppage of work, training or illness, you must register your plan with the SUB program. This program summary will help you understand the requirements of the program and how to register your plan.

Supplemental unemployment benefit (SUB) plans were introduced in 1956 as a means of supplementing employees' income during temporary layoffs due to shortage of work. This created an incentive for employees to return to work for their employer, thus reducing retraining and other costs associated with hiring new employees.

In response to the needs of the private sector and in keeping with the intent of Canadian social security legislation, the criteria required to register SUB plans have subsequently been adjusted. The plans can now supplement employment insurance (EI) benefits paid for temporary stoppage of work, training, illness, injury or quarantine. SUB plans must be approved by the Department of Human Resources and Skills Development Canada (HRSDC) to ensure that payments are not considered as earnings for EI purposes and are not deducted from EI benefits.

Approximately 3,000 employers across Canada have approved SUB plans, and more than 887,500 workers benefit from these payments.

Advantages of a Supplemental Plan

The employer provides supplemental payments to increase the employee's revenue while receiving EI maternity, parental or compassionate care benefits. The supplement is not insurable; therefore, EI premiums are not deducted.

The supplement is not deducted from EI benefits if the plan meets the following two conditions:

- When the payment is added to the employee's EI weekly benefits, it does not exceed the employee's normal weekly wage earnings (100 percent of gross salary).
- The payment is not used to reduce other accumulated employment benefits, such as banked sick leave, vacation leave credits or severance pay.

The supplement can be paid during the EI waiting period without affecting the start of the EI benefits.

Is Registration of the Plan Required?

The employer is not required to obtain formal approval from Human Resources and Skills Development Canada (HRSDC) for his plan used to supplement EI maternity, parental or compassionate care benefits. Records still have to be kept to show the effective date of the plan and that it meets the two conditions.

What to Show on the Record of Employment (ROE)

When completing the ROE, the employer must indicate in the "comments" section or in an accompanying letter that a maternity, parental or compassionate care supplement will be paid and that the two conditions are met.

Information for Employees

During the period when the maternity, parental or compassionate care benefits are paid, the employee must not be required to work for the employer to repay the value of these supplements. If work is performed during that period, the employee must declare the money received, which may be deducted from his or her EI benefits.

The employee who will receive a supplement will have to indicate it in his application for maternity, parental or compassionate care benefits.

Additional Requirements

Additional requirements may be added to the employer's plan providing it does not affect the two conditions. For example, the plan may require that the employee return to work for the employer for a period of at least six months after the maternity, parental or compassionate care benefits have been paid.

THE LONG-TERM DISABILITY CLAIM

The Process of Getting Paid

First and foremost, all information provided to the insurance carrier regarding a claim is held in the strictest confidence. The process described below may vary depending upon the provider of this coverage.

There are liability issues to consider with any disability. Even if you do not offer a long-term disability benefit option within your company, as a business, you should have a corporate policy in place that states that should an employee be absent from work due to a disability, how long will that member remain on the benefit plan for the health, prescription drugs, vision and dental benefits (if applicable)? Will this be for six months or a year? This should be established well in advance so all employees are aware. In fact, each new hire should be given this as part of his or her new hire kit. As well, they should also be made aware how long will their position be held in the event of a disability and a subsequent recovery. This type of policy should be drawn up by the company's corporate lawyer and is intended as protection against any liability issues that they employee may make if he or she becomes disabled.

The Long-Term Disability Claim

The insurance company receives a claim from an employee member. This means the completed claim form (usually three parts: one for the employee to complete, one for the employer and the "Attending Physician's Statement") is returned to the insurance company to begin the process.

These are the first documents that the insurance company needs to assess the claim. In many cases, additional information is required. This can include:

- A completed report from the doctor giving relevant medical history and evidence that supports the diagnosis, as well as an explanation of how the medical condition prevents the claimant from performing his or her duties at work
- If the claimant is seeing more than one doctor, a completed report from each may be required
- Test results
- Copies of hospital records

Acknowledgment of the Claim

The insurance company will acknowledge receipt of the claim by letter to the plan member. If there is any missing information, it will be outlined in this letter.

Examination of Medical Information

The insurance company will then examine all medical information to determine if they can make a decision on the member's claim or if they need further medical information.

At this point a couple of things may occur:

1. The insurance company may request additional information from the treating physician. The member may be asked to give consent via an authorization form so this can be done directly and more expediently with the doctor.
2. An independent medical examination, by a specialist chosen by the insurance carrier, may be arranged to reassess the condition. This is done at no cost to the plan member. All necessary travel expenses are reimbursed. This examination may be necessary to properly complete the medical evaluation for a decision on the claim.

Things to note:

- All independent medical specialists are not employees of the insurance company. They are medical specialists selected because their field of medical expertise is relevant to the member's case. They are hired to conduct an objective assessment of the condition.
- Because it isn't always possible to find medical specialists to conduct these examinations in all communities and regions, the insurance carrier may ask that the member travel to see that specialist in the region where it is available.

3. At this point, the claim can be either approved or denied.

Claim Decision

The insurance carrier will notify the member in writing of the claim decision.

If the claim is denied, the plan member can ask the treating physician to provide any new additional medical information that is relevant, and the claim may be appealed for reconsideration.

If the medical information is found to be sufficient and the claim is approved, the long-term disability benefits will be paid. The insurance carrier will explain the benefit payment in the approval letter. Please note that the benefit may be reduced by the amount of any other disability income the plan member may receive, including CPP and QPP benefits.

Disability Benefits

Each policy is different, and the following is a generic description only of the eligibility for benefits once approved:

- The plan member must show the insurance carrier that he or she is unable to perform the substantial essential duties of the job due to the illness or disability.

- After a period of time, the member must show the insurance company that the medical condition prevents the member from performing any job at or above a certain earnings level.
- A member may be declined benefits due to a preexisting medical condition.
- If the member does qualify for long-term disability benefits, and it is later determined that the medical condition has improved, so that the member is no longer disabled, the benefits will cease.
- All benefits cease at age 65.

Rehabilitation Services

Once approved for long-term disability benefits, the member may receive rehabilitation counseling services from an independent professional if it is felt that these services would assist the member in his or her efforts to return to work.

In coordinating the return-to-work efforts, the counselor may meet with the treating physicians and the employer. The counselor may involve other professionals to provide assessments, support and rehabilitation programs where necessary. Financial support for vocational or other educational programs may be made available in cases where the counselor and the insurance company considers them to be necessary for the member to return to work.

If the member participates in an approved program of rehabilitative employment, the long-term disability benefit will be reduced only when the benefits (including other disability income) and earnings from employment together exceed the percentage of the predisability earnings as specified in the plan policy.

Reporting Employee Status

It is important in all cases to keep the insurance companies up-to-date with regard to employees' status within the company. Keeping employees' records up-to-date is critical to the administration of the benefit plan.

Such updates would include the following:

- Employees who have applied for disability coverage but have been declined and have not returned to work.
- Employees who have been receiving disability benefits but who are no longer considered disabled according to the definition of disability and have not returned to work.
- When the plan member returns to work, a notice of return to work form should be completed and sent into the insurance carrier.
- When the employee is no longer covered for any benefits under the plan and should be terminated.

THE DISABILITY TAX CREDIT

Always Consult Your Accountant

If you are a person with a disability or you support someone with a disability, you may be able to claim, on your tax return the deductions and tax credits listed below:

Line 215—Disability Supports Deduction

If you have a mental or physical impairment, you may be able to deduct certain disability support expenses paid that allowed you to work, go to school or do research.

This line was previously called "attendant care expenses." Under proposed legislation, this deduction has been replaced with a broader disability supports deduction. There are now other disability supports expenses you can claim at this line in addition to attendant care expenses. Also, you no longer need to qualify for the disability amount to be eligible for this deduction unless you are claiming part-time attendant care expenses.

Line 306—Amount for Infirm Dependents Age 18 or Older

If you are eligible for this amount, you can claim an amount for each dependent who is 18 years of age or older.

Completing the Tax Return

If you are eligible to claim the amount for infirm dependents age 18 or older, for each of your dependents, calculate his or her net income (line 236 on the return, or the amount that it would be if he or she filed a return). If your dependent's net income for 2004 was $9,152 or more, you cannot make a claim.

Note that you should have a signed statement from a medical doctor that gives the nature, commencement date and duration of the dependent's infirmity. Keep the statement. Your claim can be reduced if you cannot show it later.

Claims made by more than one person: If you and another person support the same dependent, you can split the claim for that dependent. However, the total of your claim and the other person's claim cannot be more than the maximum amount allowed for that dependent.

You can claim an amount for each of your or your spouse or common-law partner's dependent children or grandchildren only if that child or grandchild was:

- mentally or physically infirm; and
- born in 1986 or earlier.

You can also claim an amount for more than one person as long as each one meets all of the following conditions. The person must have been

- your or your spouse's or common-law partner's brother, sister, niece, nephew, aunt, uncle, parent or grandparent;
- born in 1986 or earlier;
- mentally or physically infirm;
- dependent on you, or on you and others, for support; and
- a resident of Canada at any time in the year.

You cannot claim this amount for a person who was only visiting you.

Note: A child can include someone older than you who has become dependent on you.

If, for a particular dependent, anyone other than you is claiming an amount on line 305 or anyone (including you) can claim an amount on line 315, you cannot claim an amount on line 306 for that dependent. If you are claiming an amount on line 305 for a dependent who is infirm and age 18 or older, you also may be able to claim a part of the amount on line 306 for that dependent.

You can claim an amount only if the dependent's net income (line 236 of their return, or the amount that it would be if he or she filed a return) is less than $9,152.

If you were required to make support payments for that child, you cannot claim an amount on line 306 for that child. However, if you were separated from your spouse or common-law partner for only part of 2004 due to a breakdown in your relationship, you can still claim an amount for that child on line 306 (plus any allowable amounts on line 305 and line 318) as long as you do not claim any support amounts paid to your spouse or common-law partner on line 220. You can claim whichever is better for you.

Which Expenses Are Eligible?

The following amounts are eligible, if you used that particular service or device because of your impairment:

- amounts paid for sign-language interpretation services or real-time captioning services used by individuals who have a speech or hearing impairment (and paid to persons in the business of providing such services);
- amounts paid for teletypewriters or similar devices that enable individuals with a speech or hearing impairment to make and receive telephone calls, if prescribed by a medical practitioner;
- amounts paid for devices or equipment designed to be used only by blind individuals operating a computer—such as a Braille printer or large-print on-screen device, if prescribed by a medical practitioner;
- amounts paid for optical scanners or similar devices designed for use by blind individuals to enable them to read print, if prescribed by a medical practitioner; and
- amounts paid for electronic speech synthesizers that enable individuals with a speech impairment to communicate by using a portable keyboard, if prescribed by a medical practitioner.

In addition, the following may also be eligible for the deduction if a medical practitioner has certified, in writing, your need for those services or devices:

- amounts paid for note-taking services used by individuals with mental or physical impairments (and paid to persons in the business of providing such services);
- amounts paid for voice-recognition software used by individuals with a physical impairment;
- amounts paid for tutoring services used by individuals with a learning disability or a mental impairment (and paid to persons in the business of providing such services);
- amounts paid for talking textbooks used by individuals with a perceptual disability in connection with the individual's enrollment at a secondary school in Canada or designated educational institution; and
- amounts paid for full-time attendant care services provided in Canada, used by individuals with a mental or physical infirmity. Only individuals who qualify for the disability amount (see line 316) can claim amounts paid for part-time attendant care as a disability supports deduction. Amounts paid for attendant care services provided by the taxpayer's spouse or common-law partner, or to individuals under 18 years of age, do not qualify for the deduction.

DISABILITY WHILE ON MATERNITY

Most short- and long-term disability plans will now cover the part of maternity leave that the woman would not be able to work due to pregnancy and child birth health-related reasons.

Maternity and parental leaves of absence are made available to adoptive and birth parents to provide new parents with time to adjust to the new role as parents.

Federal government employment insurance supports this goal by paying benefits to new parents while they are away from work.

Why Coverage Is Available

In the last few years, there has been growing awareness that while a woman is on maternity leave, there may be a period of time during which she may be unable to work due to the physical demands of pregnancy and childbirth. She could therefore be eligible for disability benefits.

In September 2001, Ontario's Employment Standards Act introduced a new regulation requiring plan sponsors with disability plans to provide disability coverage during maternity leave.

Although not yet challenged across Canada, the Human Rights Commissions in some provinces has already indicated they would support such a claim.

For these reasons, many insurance carriers will provide disability coverage during the health-related portion of maternity leave. (Please check with your particular insurance provider to ensure that this is their policy as well.)

Limitations: To be eligible for short- or long-term disability during maternity leave, the following conditions must be met.

Coverage must be in force at the time of disability: In some provinces, a woman is able to choose whether to continue her benefit plan while on maternity or parental leave. If coverage is discontinued and the disability period starts after her leave begins, the disability will not be covered.

The disability must be the result of pregnancy or childbirth: if the woman becomes disabled for other reasons or is injured during her maternity leave, she is considered to be on leave of absence, and the plan's provisions for leave of absence will apply.

The plan's disability waiting period and all other contract requirements must be satisfied.

How this affects the plan: This change is expected to have a minor impact on the plan's disability costs.

Claims for disability benefits during maternity leave should be submitted in the same manner as all other disability claims, and the adjudication process will not change.

Disability Definitions

What Does It Mean to Be Disabled?

Individual disability contracts have three basic definitions of *total disability*.

1. Any Occupation

Employees are considered to be disabled if they cannot perform the substantial duties of their own occupation, are not gainfully employed elsewhere and cannot do anything for which they have been educated or trained or in which they have work experience.

This is the most restrictive definition of *total disability*.

2. Regular Occupation

This employee is disabled if he or she cannot perform the substantial duties of his or her occupation and is not gainfully employed elsewhere.

This is more liberal than the "any occupation" definition of *total disability*. Employees will receive benefits as long as they are disabled based on their occupation. However, if employees decide to work elsewhere, the claim will cease.

3. Own Occupation

Employees are disabled if they cannot perform the substantial duties of their own occupation.

This is the most liberal definition of *total disability*. Employees receive full benefits when they cannot work in their regular occupation, even though they are working elsewhere and earning an income.

The definition of *total disability* is the most important feature of any disability contract.

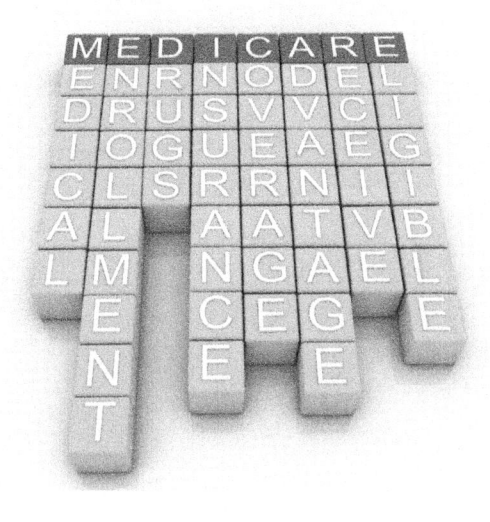

Section 6

Experience Rated Benefits
Pharmacy
Extended Health Care
Vision Care
Dental Care
Employee Assistance
Health Spending Accounts
Administrative Services Only

THE MULTIPLE TIERS OF HEALTH CARE

Health Care Coverage

Two-tier heath care—these are buzzwords for any news story talking about the ever-increasing costs of providing health care in Canada.

Acrimony accompanies the words two-tier health care. Seems like there is always a lot of opposition to the concept, equating two-tier health to the private versus the public system.

Opposition to two-tier health care? Hmm. I can't quite wrap my head around it since, in my opinion, as a benefit broker, we live in a country where multiple levels of health care already exist and coexist.

Tier 1: The base public system. Coverage for general practitioner doctors' visits and emergency, hospital services, among other items.

Tier 2: Worker's compensation for employees injured on the job. Direct, fast and full access to treatment immediately to get the employee back into the workforce.

Tier 3: Employee group benefits, providing coverage (based on company choice) for life insurance, disability, pharmacy, professional health services, vision care and dental care, none of which would be covered in any of the other two tiers mentioned.

Tier 4: Private professional services purchased directly by an individual

There certainly could be other "tiers" not mentioned. The point is, are the majority of Canadians not in opposition to what is already in existence yet creating artificial barriers to health success? Or is that the majority of the population is only opposed to private health clinics when it does not apply to them personally?

Put another way, if an employee injured his or her back on the job, falling within the realm of workers' compensation, should that person be expected to stand in the same line waiting for an appointment with the back specialist as those who have injured their backs outside of the confines of the job?

Should an employee injured at work jump the queue to see a specialist, get the MRI and get back to work faster than the person who injured his or her back on the weekend moving furniture?

By all accounts, these two individuals are equal in every way except where they incurred their injury. Should those incapacitated outside the confines of work be penalized or unable to seek private treatment to take control of their own outcomes and ensure that they too get back to work in a timely fashion simply because they were not injured on the job?

Considering how some provinces ban private insurance for publicly insured services to inhibit queue jumping and preserve the fairness of the health-care system, why then are those under the auspice of workers' compensation allowed to do so?

Food for thought.

INTRODUCTION TO PRESCRIPTION DRUG COVERAGE IN CANADA

Canadians have access to three main types of coverage for their prescription needs. They may be able to access government-funded programs, such as the Alberta Non-Group, etc., individual health insurance, personal insurance or employee group benefit plans offered through their work.

Generally speaking, drug coverage from employee benefits is less restrictive than individual programs and is not subject to preexisting conditions.

Subject to predefined exclusions, an eligible pharmaceutical must

1. be prescribed by a physician, dentist or psychiatrist,
2. be medically necessary, and
3. have an associated DIN (drug identification number).

Depending on the plan's definitions for coverage, though the drug may meet the definitions above, it may still be excluded from coverage, as with the following:

- Lifestyle drugs, such as smoking cessation aids, fertility, weight loss, and contraceptive drugs
- New drugs that have just been approved for public use (i.e., are just out of clinical trials)
- Brand-name drugs if there is an equivalent generic drug
- Over-the-counter medications

4. Medical marijuana (it is not yet covered by personal health insurance plans; however, there are some employee benefits plans that do offer some coverage for marijuana that is prescribed by a physician)

However, the following drugs are never covered by private health insurance:

- Medications that are not prescribed (e.g. over-the-counter drugs).
- Medicines administered in a hospital (these are covered by your provincial healthcare plan).
- Prescription drugs that do not have a DIN number.

A drug identification number (e.g., DIN) is an eight-digit identification number assigned by Health Canada to all drugs sold in Canada, including prescription drugs. This number provides information such as the drug manufacturer, the name of the drug, active ingredients, etc. The DIN is always displayed somewhere within the drug container's label and would be listed on the receipt from the pharmacist.

Generic Substitution

Many health insurance plans will not cover the costs of a proprietary, brand-name prescription drug if there is a generic equivalent drug available. (Note that generic drugs are substantially cheaper compared to equivalent brand name prescription drugs.)

Specialty Drug Coverage Programs

Each province in Canada has its own specialty prescription drug programs that tend to be for either senior citizens or low-income families.

Understanding Drug Pooling

How are the pharmacy claims addressed for employee treatments of consistent, ongoing, expensive drug treatment, which runs anywhere from $40,000 to $80,000 a year?

A portion of the claim falls under the experience of the benefits plan, but the vast majority is "pooled" within the industry as a whole—pure insurance. Think of it like purchasing home insurance and your home burns to the ground. When your home is replaced, you wouldn't expect the rates to reflect the full replacement costs. The high-risk claims are "pooled" among other insured people to spread the exposure of risk.

In that same manner, the insurance industry's drug-pooling framework ensures recurring high-cost drug claims are brought together to allow movement of business, increase plan sustainability and mitigate risk.

Industry Drug-Pooling Framework

In 2013, the Canadian Life and Health Insurance Association (CLHIA)—the not-for-profit membership organization representing the insurance industry—worked to establish a framework for insurers to pool recurring high-cost drug claims. They established the Canadian Drug Insurance Pooling Corporation (CDIPC) to administer this plan for the industry.

Drug pooling is essential to the sustainability of claims of this nature. The following are some highlights scooped from Green Shield's information posting.

- Participating insurers place eligible high-cost drug claims from all of their fully insured group drug plans into their own proprietary pools called extended drug policy protection plans or EP3s.
- Insurers set premiums for the plan sponsor's fully insured drug plans without including any pooled high-cost drug claims experience.
- When the costs exceed the initial threshold specified by CDIPC for two consecutive calendar years, the industry drug pool

supports the EP3 by removing much of the effect of high-cost recurrent drug claims.
- In the background, the participating insurers spread the cost of the high-cost claims among all of the insurers by putting the claims into an industry-wide drug pool administered by CDIPC—this spreads the risk of recurring high-cost claims across all of the insurers.

Utilizing pooling to the benefit of all means employers don't have to resort to restricting reimbursement for high-cost drugs. And in turn, plan members should continue to receive coverage even when their plan is incurring ongoing high-cost drug claims. This has created a greater degree of consistency regarding managing the costs of drugs below the industry pool threshold.

Why Care?

With the premium rates being applied are a portion specified to cover these "pooling" charges. When analyzing the renewal rate structure, it is important to note that the rates themselves may be increasing not based on your own usage within the group of employees housed under that benefit plan, but also funding the pool for those "just-in-case" catastrophic drug claims, as well as those established ongoing claims already in process within the pool.

For employers, these rates represent the cost of the claims within the EP3. Due to the fact that the financials behind the framework are complex, plan sponsors may not necessarily consider the pooling charges forming part of the premium. Though this varies, pooling typically starts between $10,000 and $15,000 and then enters the industry drug pool at the threshold of $32,500 to a maximum pooling amount of half a million dollars covered by all insurers through CDIPC. Remember, the insurer is prohibited from experience rating these claims.

Industry experts continue to emphasize drug pooling on its own was never intended as a long-term solution to very high-priced pharmaceutical, simply to buy additional time to develop a more comprehensive solution.

Consider that without the pooling framework, some plans would have had to halt access to coverage, which obviously would have had negative effects. The high cost of drugs is definitely a bigger societal issue that, as time goes on, is becoming more urgent to tackle.

DRUGS

Prescription Drug Coverage

A constant in the group insurance arena is how to combat the increasing costs of prescriptions but ensure employees continue to receive the coverage they need. Before a strategy to combat these increasing costs can be implemented, it is imperative to understand why the costs are increasing.

It is one thing to stipulate that according to current statistics, annual drug spending per employee should increase in double digits. Getting to the "why" is more beneficial when building strategy.

Every year, new drugs are introduced and new drug therapies. Biologic drugs are becoming more mainstream and cost substantially more than traditional drug therapies. As some drugs lose their patent exclusivity, leading to the introduction of low-price generic equivalents, these costs are offset somewhat, but the fact of the matter is that we have an aging demographic and the "need" for these treatments continue to monopolize the funds allocated to benefits, resulting in double-digit plan cost increases.

With the top 1 percent of claimants utilizing more than 30 percent of the benefit, where's the good news? Well, 85 percent of people who utilize pharmaceuticals claim less than $2,000 per year. Understand that younger employees aged 21 to 30 are making larger claims for mental health therapies. Expected claims patterns are being turned on their ear.

But there are options and plenty of them. Analyzing to understand the metrics of the benefit plan is the first step. Implementing wellness programs such as employee assistance, which costs a mere fraction of what a drug benefit costs will assist with education and overall better health strategies. The cost of prevention is a long-term investment strategy that will pay dividends long term both in money not spent and a successful, healthy workforce.

VALUE OF STOP-LOSS

Covering for the Unforeseen Risk

The purpose of any insurance is to mitigate risk, and group insurance is no exception.

Imagine, if you would, an employee who earns $56,000 a year, has hepatitis C and has been prescribed Harvoni at a cost of $69,910 for nine rounds of treatment. For all intents and purposes, when this employee completes the prescribed rounds, he or she will be cured, and the benefit plan will have done its job in offering a true benefit to this employee.

Hep C is just one of several costly medical conditions employees in any income level and of any race, gender or geographic location can suffer from. Those with rheumatoid arthritis, cancer and multiple sclerosis are now being prescribed medications that cost in excess of $30,000 a year every year.

But wait—that's $69,910 in costs to the prescription side of the benefit plan. Won't the rates only escalate to recover that cost?

No.

That's why stop-loss provisions are built into the benefit plan.

Stop-loss insurance is designed to protect employers against sudden, unexpected, catastrophic risk. Claims in excess of the stop-loss deductible per person per year (in this case $10,000) are insured and do not count against the employer's experience when setting health-care budgets for future renewals. This limits the employer's risk while enabling continued coverage and protection for employees through the benefits plan.

The true cost of the employer's experience was the $10,000 for this one claim. That's close to a $60,000 gain on the investment into that employee's health.

Consider this: had this employee not had access to a benefit plan, he or she would not have been able to financially access the cure required and, in all likelihood, would have gone untreated only to develop further life-threatening conditions, such as liver disease or cancer of the liver.

ENTITLEMENT

Pooling for High Claims

Are we entitled?

Consider this—we live in a country where we expect to be taken care of without ever having to ante up to pay the bill. We assume these expenses should be covered either through government programs or employee group benefit plans.

Without a doubt, advances in medicine have brought many life-saving drugs—and hope—to people suffering from serious health problems. At the same time, new ways to diagnose illness—sooner—are being developed. So are new treatment guidelines, which help control disease more effectively. The result is doctors now prescribe drugs sooner than they did in the past, and Canadians are taking more drugs than ever before. While these treatments improve life and sustain a healthy and contributing workforce, these drugs are costly, putting additional pressure on employee benefit plans.

This additional pressure can be seen with the rate increases annually. How many renewals have I presented in the last year alone where the claims far surpassed the premiums paid—in some cases two to three times—yet no one wants to pay more in premium? I get it. I'm right there with you. For sure when that employee with multiple sclerosis requires Gilenya at a cost of more than $30,000 annually, we expect the benefit plan will pay for it—but with no increase to the premium. Why?

Though the rates may increase, they are certainly not increasing to the levels to cover the additional expenses. Why? Because the plan is insured.

This brings us to the purpose of insurance—to mitigate risk. It is for these high claims that stop-loss protection, or pooling, is in place. The claims experience is moved into the pool. What this means is expenditures in excess more than the pooling limit (typically $10,000) are not considered for the experience for the group. So where does the claims experience go? Who's in charge of the pool? Who pays the bill?

In 2013, on fully insured plans, the Canadian Drug Insurance Pooling Corporation (CDIPC) began requiring the inclusion of pooling protection in the form of an Extended Healthcare Policy Protection Plan (EP3).

However, the CDIPC guidelines stipulate that self-insured, Administrative Services Only (ASO) plans are not eligible to have high-cost claims pooled in an EP3.

This healthcare pooling protects the plan from high claims. Once the combined claims of an employee—and his or her eligible dependents, if any—go higher than the specified amount, the claims become fully pooled. These costs are not reflected in benefit rate. Instead, clients are charged an annual pooling fee.

Pooling is security in numbers. Because claim costs are shared across the entire pool of clients under that insurer, customers become insulated from the full impact of any high-cost claims.

The CDIPC has set rules for all healthcare insurance carriers to follow when it comes to pooling.

BIOLOGIC

Prescription Drug Trends

It can be easily noted in the group benefit marketplace a distinct fear of biologic drugs. Accounting for millions in annual claims, this is a fear well grounded, not of their necessity, but a fear of having to pay for them out of the benefit dollars.

First, we should outline what a biologic drug is; biologics have been around for about twenty years or so and are best known for their development in combating diseases like arthritis, cancer, diabetes and multiple sclerosis. The difference between a biologic drug and a typical pharmaceutical would be the shelf life. A biologic is made up of a living system (microorganism, plant or animal cell) and cannot be stored for the long term, whereas a typical pharmaceutical is chemical based and therefore can be stored for long periods of time.

Because a biologic is typically a large, complex mixture of molecules using, in many cases, recombinant DNA technology, biologics are not mass produced and are sensitive to minor changes in the manufacturing process, and this increases the costs of these drugs dramatically. Where a cost of a typical pharmaceutical may be hundreds of dollars, a biologic by contrast will be thousands of dollars per use.

According to Telus Health Solutions' 2010 research, biologic drugs represent 14 percent to 16 percent of drug spending and 60 percent of catastrophic claims. However, they account for less than 1 percent of the total number of claims, according to ESI Canada's 2009 Drug Trend Report. Biologic drug claims are growing by 14 percent per year (versus 4 percent for other drugs) and are expected to account for 33 percent of overall drug spending.

Specialty drugs in Canada cost about $132 million a year, encompassing high-cost injection and infusion drug therapies. These are high-touch, high-support, specifically distributed drug treatments, which can rack up the drug utilization on a benefit plan with just one user.

The drug Avast, for example, used in cancer treatment can cost upward of $50,000 a year. Arthritic medication costs between $20 and $30,000 per year, per patient.

The ability to claim for these drugs is a concern from both access and cost perspectives. No one wants to be denied access; however, employers are rightly concerned about what to do with the costs. Moving into these new innovative therapies means everyone has responsibility to be involved to make the treatment successful and affordable.

To put biologic advancement in perspective, there are more than six thousand rare diseases right now, yet there are only treatments for about four hundred, with another two thousand rare treatments in development.

Good treatments result in less hospitalization and use of the healthcare system. So the consideration comes down to weighing the treatment costs versus the long-term cost effectiveness of a healthier workforce.

More on the Biologic

Increased Costs, Increased Liability

Biologic drugs have been around for about twenty years or so and are best known for their development in combating diseases like cancer, diabetes and multiple sclerosis. The difference between a biologic drug and a typical pharmaceutical would be the shelf life. A biologic is made up of a living system (microorganism, plant or animal cell) and cannot be stored for long term, whereby a typical pharmaceutical is chemical based and therefore can be stored for long periods of time.

Because a biologic is typically a large, complex mixture of molecules using, in many cases recombinant DNA technology, biologics are not mass produced and are sensitive to minor changes in the manufacturing process, and this increases the costs of these drugs dramatically.

Where a cost of a typical pharmaceutical may be hundreds of dollars, a biologic by contrast will be thousands of dollars per use.

According to many research studies, biologic drugs represent 14 percent to 16 percent of drug spending and 60 percent of catastrophic claims and are growing by about 14 percent per year (versus 4 percent for other drugs).

Specialty drugs in Canada costs about $132 million a year, encompassing high-cost injection and infusion drug therapies. These are high-touch, high-support, specifically distributed drug treatments, which can rack up the drug utilization on a benefit plan with just one user.

The drug Avast, for example, used in cancer treatment can cost upward of $50,000 a year. Humors, an arthritis medication, costs between $20,000 to $30,000 per year, per patient.

Covering these drugs is a concern from both access and cost perspectives. No one wants to be denied access; however, employers are rightly concerned about what to do with the costs. Moving into these new innovative therapies means everyone has responsibility to be involved to make the treatment successful and affordable.

To put biologic advancement in perspective, there are more than six thousand rare diseases right now, yet there are treatments for about four hundred, with another two thousand rare treatments in development.

Good treatments result in less hospitalization and use of the healthcare system; therefore, although the initial treatment is costlier, over the long term it will be more cost effective.

GENERIC DRUGS

A Drug by Any Other Name

An interesting question came up about generic drugs at a recent seminar; would generic drugs be more acceptable to patients if they were called something other than generic?

I likened this question to Coke's foray into changing the colour of the can from red to white for their polar bear theme during Christmas. Due to mass rejection, Coke recalled the cans. The inside—the soda—was exactly the same. So what's the problem?

Perception.

Loyal customers rejected the change in can colour, saying the soda tasted different in the white can.

Generic drugs have been available in Canada since 1969. Despite their availability in the marketplace for almost a half century, patients continue to consider generics substandard. Interestingly enough, the generic "name" is set upon inception of the pharmaceutical as depicted by the identical chemical makeup of the drug. It is, in fact, the chemical name of the drug. The brand name, as it were, is set after the invention of the drug as the marketable (salable) name.

A generic drug must meet the same rigorous standards as the brand name set by the health protection branch of the federal government. A generic may more aptly be named the "bio equivalent," as that is indeed what they are by definition. What this means is that they have to work exactly the same as the brand name drug. There is less than a 5 percent difference between the brand name and generic drugs therapies.

A patient may well consider this option the same as purchasing tissue or Kleenex. Kleenex is a brand name, yet we may purchase another brand and call it Kleenex.

Not only are generic quality medications, but they also are typically produced in the same facility, are checked for quality standards and must work in the same manner as brand-name drugs, including the safety equivalent, with the same therapeutic and adverse effects.

Having generic availability on a benefit plan gives plan members options, removing unproductive expenses, as bio-equivalent drugs or bio substitutes save Canadians more than a billion dollars annually.

So the question becomes, does Coke taste the same in the white can as it does in the red can? And do you purchase Kleenex or tissues? Your answer may save you significantly on your plan costs.

MANDATORY GENERIC

Pharmacy Definitions

On a group benefit plan, there is often a lot of concern surrounding pharmacy coverage and the availability of brand name prescriptions over having to choose a mandatory generic substitution for your prescription medication needs.

What's best, and will this provide the same results if I accept the substitution?

Good questions.

In Canada, brand-name drugs have a 20-year patent protection. During this time, only the patent holder can produce the drug. After this time is up, other manufacturers may apply to Health Canada to produce generic versions. When Health Canada provides approval, governments, private insurance plans and consumers can benefit from the lower-costing pharmaceutical.

Generics could best be described as a copycat of their brand name counterpart. They have the same active ingredients as the brand name variety and are as safe and effective to use. In addition, both generic and brand name drugs sold in Canada must be approved by the federal Health Protection Branch and must meet strict regulations established by the Food and Drug Act.

The really important difference between a brand name and a generic is price. Generics can often cost 40 to 50 percent less than a brand name. Over the last few years, provincial governments have introduced legislation that reduced the cost of generic drugs offered on provincial formularies to 18 to 25 percent of the brand name prices.

The generic variety may have a different name and look slightly different, but the quality, safety and effectiveness are equal.

When used as prescribed, generic versus the more expensive brand name drug will save valuable health-care dollars.

A "no substitution" from a doctor on a plan where mandatory generic is required involves a form completed by the patient's doctor for approval of this additional cost on the benefit plan.

DRUG IDENTIFICATION NUMBER

Why the DIN Is Necessary

When purchasing a prescription drug, you will notice an eight-digit drug identification number (DIN) on the drug label and on the formal receipt issued by the pharmacist. If a drug has a DIN, you know that Health Canada has assessed its safety and that it has been authorized for sale in Canada.

A DIN is helpful for a number of reasons. It makes it easy to follow up on drug products that are on the market, in the event they need to be inspected as part of ongoing quality monitoring or if they are facing recall. A drug product being sold in Canada without a DIN has not been approved for sale by Health Canada.

What Does It Mean to You?

Many drugs that have a DIN appear on provincial drug listings (called a formulary). Any drugs on the listing are eligible for coverage under provincial drug plans. (Some provinces have drug plans for all residents; others provide drug coverage for special groups, for example, seniors or social service recipients.)

Provincial drug listings also provide the basis for the list of drugs covered under group benefit plans. A predefined list of drugs ensures that plan members will receive the drugs that are necessary for the treatment of illness or disease. It also ensures equal treatment for all members of the plan.

Some group benefit plans may add or remove certain DINs from their drug listing to either enhance or eliminate coverage under certain drug categories. For example, stop-smoking drugs may be covered under some plans and not covered under others.

When reordering a prescription, you would normally identify the drug to your pharmacist by giving them the DIN. Pharmacists use DINs to confirm that the correct drug has been dispensed.

When you submit a drug claim to your provider, they use the DIN to identify the drug as covered under your plan.

Important things to remember

- Attach all original receipts and other documents regarding your claim. When including pharmacy receipts, be sure they show the drug identification number (DIN) and the name of the medication. A cash register receipt alone is not enough. If you're making a claim for paramedical or medical equipment expenses, the receipts you submit need to include the practitioner's registration number.
- If your claim is for the portion of expenses that your spouse's plan didn't cover, you need to include the claims statement that your spouse received from his or her plan with your claims form.

Be sure to sign your claim form. This is critical since your signature gives consent and authorization needed to process the claim. Unsigned claim forms will be returned for signature. When you resubmit the form, the claim will be processed.

THE WINDS OF CHANGE

Medical Marijuana

Medical marijuana is not currently eligible for coverage under traditional health care benefit plans as it does not have a drug identification number (DIN).

Health Canada will need to issue DIN numbers to it before insurance providers can start to determine eligibility.

For now, medical marijuana claim expenses can only be paid through cost plus (MRP) or health spending accounts (HSA).

As we are led to understand the process, in order to make a claim for medical marijuana, the receipt and prescription have to be submitted in the patient's name, as dispensed through a recognized, licensed dispensary.

In recent news, the Human Rights Board in Nova Scotia ruled that a company was discriminating against an employee by not providing coverage for his medical marijuana and ordered that it be covered.[4]

The decision was specific to this particular individual and case, and there are no planned changes to GWL's position with respect to coverage of medical marijuana under their drug plans. Their standard response to inquiries on medical marijuana coverage remains as follows:

> The medical marijuana environment continues to evolve and Great-West Life is actively monitoring developments in this area. Health Canada continues to maintain their position that marijuana is not an approved drug and has

---

[4] http://www.benefitscanada.com/news/benefits-plan-must-cover-medical-marijuana-rules-n-s-human-rights-commission-rules-93415?utm_source=Email-Marketing&utm_medium=email&utm_campaign=Daily_Newsletter.

not granted a drug identification number (DIN). Given the Health Canada position, as well as other regulatory and distribution challenges, Great-West Life does not consider expenses for medical marijuana as eligible under any of the current drug plans.

Alternatively, the Canada Revenue Agency deems expenses for medical marijuana as eligible under the Medical Expense Tax Credit meaning that those expenses could be considered eligible under a Health Care Spending Account.

LIFE AFTER POT

What will it mean?

Medical marijuana has become a consistent element of discussion under a group benefit plan these last years. With the availability of being able to process claims for medical marijuana under a health spending account, it is only a matter of time where the access of coverage under the mainstream—core—benefit package becomes the norm. The reason medical marijuana is not included in health plans is because Health Canada has still not issued it a drug identification number (DIN).

The end of the prohibition for recreational use by the federal government enables anyone over the age of 18 to purchase up to 30 grams of dried or fresh cannabis. In two separate bills, the Liberals plan to regulate the recreational side, as well as impose stringent measures against impaired driving. Because provinces will be responsible for distribution and sale, they also have the power to increase the minimum age if they see fit.

As cannabis use becomes more normalized in the years to come, it is likely Canada's main providers will come on board. But with the high costs of drugs being an issue, segmenting and encouraging overall maximums and applied health-related situations, such as only allowing the usage to treat certain illnesses, such as cancer, multiple sclerosis and the like, may be necessary to curb escalating costs.

BEST DOCTORS

The Remote Expert Second Opinion

Better outcomes start with the right diagnosis.

Best Doctors is dedicated to improving quality of care by helping make sure individuals get the right diagnosis and the right treatment. The Best Doctors consultation program harnesses the expertise of the exclusive Best Doctors database, bringing the clinical knowledge of some of the world's most respected experts to the problems of patients with serious illnesses.

Best Doctors helps improve the quality of care for seriously ill individuals by answering two basic questions: Is the diagnosis correct? What is the best treatment?

By making sure employees get the right care, Best Doctors reduces complications and helps avoid and ineffective treatment. Best Doctors helps employers contain health-care costs by empowering employees with information to make the best choices.

Best Doctors solves medical cases, not by moving the individual or switching doctors but by having leading experts actively consult on a case and interact with the treating doctors. The exhaustive analysis of each case helps make sure the individual gets the right diagnosis and the right treatment. Impressively, statistics demonstrate that the intervention of Best Doctors has resulted in a revised diagnosis 22 percent of the time and a revised treatment plant 61 percent of the time.

Second opinions focus on alternative treatment plans for particular cases. The InterConsultation program focuses first on the medical decisions made by the treating doctors to determine if the initial diagnosis is correct. Then by working doctor to doctor, the InterConsultation program helps ensure that the right treatment decisions are made and that there is the best chance for optimal outcome.

The two main goals of Best Doctors are as follows: (1) to help individuals and physicians identify and access the best care available and improve medical outcomes by harnessing the power of that expertise and (2) to integrate Best Doctors services into employee benefit plans to help identify cases where Best Doctors can help better manage serious medical events by providing reliable, actionable clinical knowledge and optimal treatment pathways.

"Without a question, the most significant impact to date has been a high level of expertise provided by best doctors. Our retrospective analysis found that this program saved $287,567 per average case on acute medical costs and 67.3 percent of patients avoided one or more invasive surgical procedures."[5]

The business of Best Doctors is a clinical expertise. They are the only company that harnesses the knowledge of more than 50,000 doctors identified by their peers to be the best in their specialties. By combining the skill, experience and insight of these highly trained doctors, Best Doctors is able to deliver on unparalleled medical resources that results in better medical care at lower costs.

Some insured benefit plans currently offer this benefit as part of the Extended Health Care Program (limited to Great-West Life).

Individuals can join on their own at a cost of $90 per year or $180 per year for a family, or a company can purchase this a benefit on a group basis at a discounted price.

---

[5] Bruce G. Sundquist, Vice President Claims, American Re-Insurance Company (2005 results based in 465 cases analyzed by American Re-Insurance Company since April 2001).

INFLUENZA

Taking Care of Employees and Their Families

It's always fun to return to work from the bliss of the holidays in January to find yourself in the thick of sniffle and cough season, otherwise known as influenza. Despite the historical data of the flu's contributing influence in causing death, people continue to treat the condition as being no worse than a bad cold.

Primarily a respiratory virus, influenza can rear its green-goo head as early as October and last well into April or May, peaking typically in February or March. Worldwide, the flu is responsible for more than 250,000 deaths annually. It is certainly not a condition to take lightly, especially when the flu shot is so widely available.

Common symptoms include:

- Fever
- Body and muscle aches
- Cough (usually dry)
- Headache
- Fatigue or exhaustion
- Weakness

Though nothing can guarantee immunity, protection and precaution are key.

The flu vaccine is recommended for nearly everyone six months of age and older. This can be in the form of a shot, nasal spray or intradermal vaccine.

Handwashing may seem simple enough, but it is amazing how many people don't wash often enough or correctly. This can unwittingly spread the germs to others. Handwashing isn't about the soap killing the germs. The lather, friction and eventual rinsing are the mechanisms that that wash the germs away.

At the heart of any form of healthy living is diet and exercise. Flu prevention is no exception. Staying healthy keeps the immune system strong and able to fight against exposure. This includes getting enough sleep, allowing the body to rest and heal effectively.

At the height of flu season, hand sanitizer and distance are critical to fight against the constant exposure. Though tough, when interaction with people who are ill is unavoidable, be sure to wash right away and encourage children to cough or sneeze into their elbows instead of their hands.

Cleanliness also includes frequently used surfaces. Influenza can live on surfaces for two to eight hours without any detectable signs. Cell phones, doorknobs, computer keyboards, children's toys and faucet handles are hotbeds of germ growth and often overlooked for constant cleaning.

If you are symptomatic, be sure to visit your doctor and note your benefit plan has been set up to take care of the cost of pharmaceutical to assist in the rapid recovery and return to a healthy state as quickly as possible.

Massage Usage on the Rise

Have a look at the latest usage trends on your benefit plan. Where health-care services used to amount to perhaps 3 percent to 8 percent of the claiming activity on a benefit program, it is now creeping up, in some instances, to rival pharmacy and dental usage depending on the demographic makeup and health of an employee group.

With the proliferation of digital access for claiming, it's easier than ever for employees to attend professional paramedical treatments, such as massage, physiotherapy and chiropractic, and not have to pay out of pocket a cent. The argument of the actual benefit health wise is to point to evidence supporting the actual relief of stress, tension or other physical aches will be left to the professionals, but in the meantime, employers are footing the bill for millions in claim dollars the last few years.

In 2016, the majority of adult Canadians (79 percent) tried at least one form of complementary or alternative medicine, according to a new report from the Fraser Institute.

From the SANOFI Canada Healthcare Survey, 43 percent of plan members submit claims for massage therapy, with the vast majority being female claimants. Those employees aged 34 and under claim more than other demographics in the group.

In addition to the rise of massage, chiropractic is up by 42 percent, followed by acupuncture, osteopathy and naturopathy. It's interesting to note that many surveys and reports consulted show actual usage corresponds to the amount eligible under a benefit plan. Health insurance covered a significant proportion of respondents' costs for massage therapy (69 percent) and chiropractic (76 percent).

STOP LOSS INSURANCE

Insurance for Catastrophic Drug Claims

The definition of insurance is risk mitigation in the face of an unforeseen catastrophic event. In employee group benefits, this would be risk of loss of life, risk of loss of income and risk of a catastrophic event. We would lump high pharmaceutical in this category.

Within an insured plan, stop-loss insurance is specifically designed to cover catastrophic prescription needs. It is intended for the high-cost, unplanned catastrophic eventualities, not the everyday antibiotic pharmaceuticals. Because no one typically chooses to be on a lifelong medication, this is coverage essential in all benefit plans.

Unlike other aspects of the health-care system, there is no universal coverage is in place for prescription drugs. Nevertheless, they are a common household expense, with millions of prescriptions filled each year—about ten for each man, woman and child.

Some current 2016 numbers for consideration:

- Prescription drug usage has increased by 9 percent since 2012.
- One percent of patients account for approximately 30 percent of the prescriptions utilized, averaging $17,000 (yes, the zeros are correct) in claims.
- A nine-round, one-time drug run for the Hepatitis C medication can cost upwards of $70,000.
- Biologic prescription use in Canada is growing at a rate of 25 percent per year, led by the following:
    ○ Anti-arthritic: Remicade, $911.8 million in sales
    ○ Liver heath: Harvoni, $615.1 million in sales

- Anti-arthritic: Humira, 581.5 million in sales
- Vision loss: Lucentis, $469.3 million in sales
- Anti-arthritic: Enbrel, $347.3 million in sales

When deciding the building blocks of the benefit plan, information is key. Strategy to support the rising costs of pharmaceuticals, as well hybrid options to mitigate claims, is critical to the planning process. This would include looking at traditional benefit models, in addition to administrative services only (ASO), ensuring stop-loss coverage is a factor of consideration and perhaps topping up, alleviating exposure with a health spending account (HSA). Segmenting a plan like this ensures accuracy in pricing for each component of the benefit plan and allows clients to see and budget their costs from one year to the next with little to no surprises, while at the same ensuring the best coverage available for their employees.

EMPLOYEE ASSISTANCE PROGRAMS (EAP)

Getting to the Root of the Problem

Estimates indicate that as much as 12 percent of the work force suffers from stress caused by personal or job-related problems. As a result, job performance can be reduced by an average of 37.5 percent. There is no question that these problems reduce an organization's productivity.

What Is an Employee Assistance Program?

The employee assistance program (EAP) is a counseling service available to employees and their dependents for aid with problems that an employee cannot seem to solve on his or her own. The EAP provides an individual with the impartial help that can make a difference. Problems are most readily resolved if detected and addressed early. The EAP is there to provide help in a confidential manner at any time, under any circumstance. The aim of the EAP is to help employees and their families lead balanced, happy and fulfilling lives at home, at work and in the communities.

Who Is Eligible?

Generally, the plan covers full-time and part-time employees and their families.

What Types of Problems Are Covered?

Counseling and consulting services are available regarding a wide variety of personal and workplace issues, which can interfere with work performance and quality of life. Included are the following:

- Personal issues (depression, worry and stress)
- Work-related issues (work stress, conflicts and burnout)
- Marital or couple issues
- Separation and divorce issues
- Abuse issues (physical, emotional, sexual)
- Family or relationship issues
- Health-related problems
- Substance misuse (alcohol, drugs, smoking, eating disorders)
- Financial strains
- Legal questions
- Career and vocational questions

When an employee or family member is confronted with these types of problems, the EAP is there to offer help.

Who Provides the Service? Where? When?

Counseling will be provided by the EAP provider network—a team of professionals with expertise in dealing with a wide range of personal, family, financial and other problems. Counseling takes place in private offices. Sessions are usually an hour in length and can be arranged day or evening at the employee's convenience

Confidentiality Assured

The cornerstone of the EAP is confidentiality. Information the employee gives through involvement with EAP will not be provided to anyone else without the employee's written authorization. All records and information received in the EAP will remain the property of the service provider.

Nothing is documented on the employee records or shared with the company or the employee's family. Employee job security or promotion opportunities cannot be jeopardized by involvement in the EAP.

Why EAP?

The first question arising is why? Why institute a program to help employees? The most basic concept is that employees with problems will be unable to work to their optimum. Studies have demonstrated that troubled employees have the following:

- Higher absenteeism
- More personal accidents, both on and off the job, and more accidents causing damage to equipment
- A greater number of sick days
- More grievances and disciplinary actions
- More morale problems
- Lower productivity
- Poorer workmanship

Depending upon the workplace, from 50 percent to 80 percent of on-the-job problems relate to problematic drinking, family disputes, finances or emotional stress.

It has been estimated that approximately 10 percent of the workforce is responsible for

- 90 percent of all discipline problems,
- 70 percent of all workers' compensation claims,
- 40 percent to 60 percent of all medical care costs, and
- 35 percent of all absenteeism.

Up to two-thirds of employees are released (terminated) from their jobs because of personal reasons. By providing assistance, management produces a more productive, safe and cost-effective workforce. Studies indicate that those employers genuinely concerned about employee welfare and with a sense of social responsibility to the community were the most apt to adopt EAPs. Enlightened employers view EAP as an investment in the human assets of the organization.

EAPs are founded on the premise that the good health of the entire workforce is a desirable goal. To maintain the healthy functioning of individuals in the work environment, and throughout their family lives, concerned management and labor can provide effective and timely assistance to troubled employees. Deteriorating job performance serves as a key indicator of the existence of behavioral or health problems, making the work site an opportune place to intervene. By promoting prevention and treatment, instead of merely disciplining employees, the chances of helping workers overcome their difficulties are further enhanced.

EAPs as Absentee Fighters

Employees who were referred to the EAP by their supervisors experienced an across-the-board improvement in job performance, especially attendance, according to a study by the San Rafael, California, based MHN.

MHN analyzed job performance ratings for 753 employees referred by a supervisor between 1989 and 1997. Supervisors were asked to rate the employees they referred on five job-performance criteria at the time of the referral and 90 days later.

Attendance was the most improved job performance factor, climbing 71 percent over the 90-day period. Scores for behavior and conduct rose 20 percent, interpersonal relationship scores went up by 13 percent, quantity of work climbed 12.5 percent and quality of work rose 9 percent over the same period. The study also found that most supervisors learned how to use the EAP from training (42 percent), the HR department (31 percent), a union representative (9 percent) or a manager (4 percent).[6]

---

[6] D. Hiatt, et al., "Effectiveness of Job Performance Referrals." *Employee Assistance Quarterly* 14, no. 4 (1999):33–43.

EMERGENCY MEDICAL ASSISTANCE

Travel Insurance

"Hi there; I'm leaving tomorrow morning for [somewhere nice and tropical with a beach], and I almost forgot—I need travel insurance!"

Why is it that something that could truly be a life-or-death situation is often the last on the travel list of things to do prior to vacationing outside of Canada?

Because people think, *It's never going to happen to me.*

Yet stories surface all the time about cases in which, if the person hadn't had the travel coverage, he or she would have been severely hooped.

The following is a true story. A young fellow in his early twenties, working full-time, booked a couple of weeks over Christmas to get away with some pals to Mexico. They were horsing around the pool at the resort, and he fell backward, landed wrong and broke his neck.

He had no travel coverage.

At the time, the travel insurance would have cost no more than $32 for those two weeks and would have provided $2 million of coverage and an interpreter and flown a family member to be with him. It would have provided accommodations and much more. In addition, the emergency medical would have seen to all of the patient's transportation, hospital and medical expenses, as well as ensured he was stabilized and returned to Canada for further treatment.

Instead, his family, worried sick here in Canada, had to foot their own bill to Mexico (as all families would), provide their own accommodations, figure out a way to get their son appropriate medical treatment, never knowing if it was the best treatment, and then get him back to Canada.

That bill went well over $100,000 that no one had sitting around under the mattress!

This young fellow will likely never work again.

Travel coverage varies from province to province, so don't assume provincial health coverage. When all things are equal, the provincial plan doesn't measure up to American or any foreign medical costs. Coverage abroad can differ depending on where you live—for example, $75 Canadian a day in hospital for British Columbians and $406 for Ontarians. Compare the average cost for emergency inpatient hospital care in the United States being more than $1,000 US a day and as high as $10,000 for intensive care!

Covering the bases means knowing what you are buying. The following are some questions for the insurance provider, whether it is a broker, travel agent or bank:

- Does the plan have a deductible that has to be paid for each claim?
- What is the policy coverage limit: $2 million or unlimited?
- Is the insurance paid out in Canadian or US dollars?
- Can the patient choose the doctor or hospital?
- Does the insurance company submit the claim directly to the provincial health plan, or is that the patient's responsibility?

Not all policies are equal.

As with all things, whether a toaster or a car, different plans offer different benefits and restrictions. One thing that can limit coverage is a preexisting condition, an ongoing or past medical problem that required consultation, prescription drugs or treatment. Travel insurers often requires a stability period where the client hasn't needed medical attention for a predetermined period prior to traveling before they will cover any expenses arising from that condition. Typically this is 60 to 90 days.

Again, this is a true event. Recently an employee called because she had been in the hospital all week and wanted travel coverage for a trip to the United States for a family reunion for the weekend after being released. After being advised that the very recent (same-day) hospitalization would mean no coverage for any complications arising out of her stay in hospital, she thought if she simply hadn't told me, she would have had coverage.

A preexisting condition or circumstance is material fact, and full disclosure is mandatory.

On the same note, most travel policies will not cover any pregnancy or childbirth complications if they occurred while traveling in the last trimester. Some won't cover any condition for which treatment was received within the six months prior to the trip: ulcers, back problems, etc.

Travel insurance is not expensive when you consider the alternative of that "just in case" event. The best holidays are worry-free.

VISION CARE

Understanding Options

Protecting your eyes and maintaining good eye health is very important. Regular eye exams and an accurate prescription can help keep your eyes in top shape.

Some benefit plans provide coverage for vision care. Check your benefits booklet to see if your plan does. Vision care benefits typically cover contact lenses and eyeglasses. Contact lenses or eyeglasses must be prescribed by an ophthalmologist or licensed optometrist and obtained from an ophthalmologist, licensed optometrist or optician.

If you have a vision care plan, it may cover some or all of the following expenses. It is important to check before making a purchase if you are not sure of your coverage.

Vision care plans may also cover the following:

- Prescription sunglasses (sunglasses that have corrective lenses)
- Laser eye-correction surgery (performed by an ophthalmologist)
- Tinting, transition lenses and hardening and photograying of lenses
- Safety goggles or safety glasses
- EasyClip (clip-on sunglasses)

In the case of "two for the price of one" or "buy one, get one" promotions, most insurers will consider the highest-cost pair for reimbursement.

The following products and services are not covered under a vision care plan:

- Accessories, including cords or cases
- Frames purchased on eBay (or other websites) or other purchases lacking receipts
- Warranty services, including buyer's protection plan
- Visual aids, such as magnifying glasses, cameras, television monitors, vision binoculars or monocular telescopes
- Clear lensectomy (a type of lens transplant performed by an ophthalmologist)

An ophthalmologist is a medical doctor trained in detecting and treating disease of the eye and performing eye surgeries.

Optometrists provide sight-testing services, and most sell their patients optical products based on the results of those testing services. Optometrists are also trained to perform eye health examinations. An optometrist refers patients to either a physician or an ophthalmologist if the patient displays conditions of the eye that are outside the range of normal. They can't perform surgery, but they often provide patients with pre- and post-surgical care. Sometimes ophthalmologists and optometrists work in the same practice and co-manage patients.

In the optical community, opticians are trained and qualified lens and frame specialists who may also, with proper training, administer free sight-testing services for specific groups of people. Their training includes dispensing eyewear, selecting frames, taking facial measurements and choosing the best lens style for the patient.

Of the three, only ophthalmologists are medical doctors.

DENTAL RECALL

Regular Checkups

Did you know?

A radio show in the 1930s established the six-month checkup. Sponsored by Pepsodent, the famous radio entertainers "Amos 'n Andy" reached 20 million people six nights a week. Typical radio commentary read, "No toothpaste can take the place of a competent dentist. Pepsodent has never been represented as a 'cure-all' or as a substitute for dental care. As dentists will tell you, Pepsodent is an able assistant in the work of keeping teeth and gums clean and healthy. They advise: Use Pepsodent twice a day. See your dentist at least twice a year."

Rationale for Extending and Maintaining the Frequency of Recall Examinations beyond Every Six Months

The six-month checkup was never based on scientific research but rather on a toothpaste commercial jingle that was popular more than 50 years ago. The Canadian Dental Association publicly acknowledged this fact in the *Journal of the Canadian Dental Association*.[7]

Rather, "the scientific basis of the 6 month dental examination has recently been challenged in the British Medical Literature. It is claimed that the oral health status of persons having less frequent visits is not markedly altered."[8]

The current consensus based on scientific evidence is that: "Informed

---

[7] *Journal of the Canadian Dental Association* 56, no. 8 (August 1990).
[8] Preventative Dental Services Practices, Guidelines and Recommendations Report, Health and Welfare Canada, 303.

consumers, especially those with no new disease over the previous one or two years, could rationally choose to extend the recall interval beyond (and with continued experience, well beyond) six months without prejudicing their Dental health in appreciable ways."[9]

Most recently, a study was carried out to compare dental health and time spent providing dental care for patients seen at 12-month and 24-month intervals. A total of 185 children ages 3 to 18 years who were at low risk for cavities participated in the two-year study. Patients were assigned randomly to 12- to 24-month recalls.

The results of this study suggest that a recall interval of 24 months is short enough to allow carious lesions to be detected before they progress to a more serious stage. It appears that short-term productivity can be increased safely by using longer recall intervals in patients at low risk for cavities.[10]

Conclusion

Current scientific research states that recall examinations for patients with low cavity risks can safely be done at 12- to 24-month intervals.

Patients with high cavity risks—children with baby bottle syndrome or enamel malformations and some third-world immigrants—are usually seen and treated under specific or emergency examinations that have no frequency limitations.

---

[9] Department of National Health and Welfare, Canada, 1988 Preventative Dental Services Report, 2nd ed., 220.

[10] Wang, Marstrander, Holst, Ovrum, and Dahl, Institute of Community Dentistry, Dental Faculty, Oslo, Norway. "Extending recall intervals—effect on resource consumption and dental health." *Community Dental Oral Epidemiology Journal* (1992).

DENTAL FEES

Lacking Consistency

In Canada, dental fees are not regulated, and dentists can set their own fees for their services. This creates a challenge for insurers, since providers need a fair and consistent basis on which to calculate claim payments. Most provincial dental associations across the country (except in Alberta) generally publish fee guides, and insurers use those fee guides to assess dental claims. That way, providers (insurance companies) can ensure that plan members are being treated equally.

Some benefit plans calculate claims based on the fee guide for the current year. Some, however, are based on a fee guide for a particular year, so the amounts covered remain the same from year to year regardless of whether subsequent fee guides increase. Refer to your benefits booklet to find out what fee guide your plan uses, and let your dentist know. Remember, you will be required to pay the difference between what the dentist charges and what your benefit plan covers.

Note: Your benefit plan covers your expenses based on the provincial fee guide for the province in which you live. If you visit a dentist in another province, your claim will be assessed based on the fee guide for your province—not the province where you received treatment.

Treatment Options

Many dental benefit plans have limits in place to ensure they are covering the most appropriate and cost-effective treatment options. The purpose of these limits is not to direct the choice of treatment; that is a matter between the patient and his or her dentist. The goal instead is to provide access to adequate dental care and at the same time keep the benefit plan affordable.

Get an Estimate

Ask your dentist about his or her fees before you receive treatments over $300. Your dental office should send your provider a fee estimate (called a predetermination) so they can let you and your dentist know, in advance, how much (if any) of the expense will be covered by your benefits plan. This simple precaution will allow you to discuss treatment options with the dentist before the work begins and to budget for the expense if it's not covered by your plan.

Note: A predetermination is not a guarantee. In some situations, the amount of benefits paid may be different than the amount that was approved when your dentist submits his or her estimate. For example:

- The actual services performed may be different from those in the fee estimate.
- Benefit plans can be changed or even terminated between the time your dentist submits the estimate and the time the work is done. If this happens, the provider will assess the claim based on the benefits in force at the time the work was done.
- Some dental plans have a limit to the overall amount they cover each year. If, between the time of the estimate and the time of your treatment, your dentist also performs other dental work, your claim for that other work will reduce the benefit amount available to cover the treatment that was approved.

More Questions about Dental Practices

What's the difference between basic/preventive services and major restorative services?

Basic/preventive services are procedures such as dental checkups, cleanings, fillings, root canals, extractions etc.

Major restorative services include crowns, bridges and dentures.

What's scaling?

Scaling (cleaning the teeth) is performed as a preventive measure during a dental checkup or when there is evidence of gum disease.

Dentists usually charge for scaling in units of time (one unit is typically 15 minutes). Your plan may limit the number of units you are allowed per year. Scaling may be covered under basic/preventive services or major restorative services, depending on your plan, so coverage may vary. Check your benefits booklet to find out what your plan covers.

Questions to Ask Your Dentist about Your Claim

What do these procedure codes mean?

Most people won't pay our mechanic until we know exactly what was fixed and why. And yet, many of us will walk out of the dentist's office without fully understanding what we've been charged for. The codes on your invoice represent specific treatment procedures that unless you're in the business, can be more than a little confusing. Many dentists provide an explanation of the codes on their invoice, but some do not.

Be sure to ask your dentist (or his or her staff) to explain exactly what the codes mean to ensure you are being charged for procedures that you actually received. If your dentist files claims electronically for you, ask for a copy and review it with them so you understand what is being claimed.

How Often Do You Need to See Your Dentist?

Depending on your teeth and dental habits, it may not be necessary to visit your dentist twice a year as the toothpaste commercials recommend. Once every nine months or even once annually might be sufficient. Talk it over with your dentist to see what's best for you. Then check your benefits booklet to see how often your plan covers checkups.

ADMINISTRATIVE SERVICES ONLY (ASO)

Understanding When to Implement ASO

Where a health spending account sets an overall maximum but opens the benefit options to anything health related, an ASO looks, acts and feels in the manner of traditional insurance; however, it is a self-funded program 100 percent paid for by the employer.

Administrative services only (ASO) is an arrangement whereby the employer provides benefits to employees on a self-insured basis and the employer purchases some or all of the administrative and claims services normally provided under an insured plan from the insurance company.

The employer assumes all of the risk or liability, and the insurance carrier administers the plan and pays claims. ASO plans are normally recommended for large groups where the claim level is predictable and are used mainly for extended health care, dental care and weekly indemnity benefits.

Under the ASO contract, the carrier will provide the following services to their clients:

- Evaluation and payment or declination of claims based on the schedule of benefits
- Investigation of claims where charges appear high
- Provision of medical advice on questionable procedures or unusually high claim amounts
- Retention of claim payment records
- Drafting of necessary forms and proposing claims submission and handling procedures

- Provision of direct claim administration, certification of claimant's eligibility and remitting of claim payments directly to the claimant
- Underwriting evidence of insurability
- Collection of funds from the employer

Claims are handled in the same way under an ASO arrangement as with an insured plan. Claims assessment and adjudication are identical except that the insurance carrier is prepared to pay an ineligible claim if directed to do so.

The employer will have to make special banking arrangements for an ASO plan since the carrier is paying claims on their behalf. The carrier will provide an accounting of the claims paid and the administration expenses are charged on the claims paid during the month.

If there is an underlying assumption that the complete cost of claims paid for by the carrier must, in the long run, be recovered from the company for whom coverage is being provided, the focus of attention then becomes centred upon minimizing the cost of delivering these benefits to employees.

An ASO arrangement can be an efficient financing vehicle to this end. We have provided a list of some of the advantages and disadvantages of the ASO arrangement.

Advantages

ASO agreements eliminate the risk borne by a carrier that a group may terminate the contract if substantial unfavorable experience occurs. The carrier expense charge for risk, within a premium structure, is therefore eliminated.

A carrier will naturally strive to accumulate reserves or profits, should favorable experience occur in a premium structure.

On a premium basis, the carrier is responsible for the incurred but not reported claims that exist for all health-care plans. This cost is built into premiums and can range from one to three months, depending on many factors. Normally, this reserve bears no interest credit for a group and can be a subject of contention on occasion between a group and their carrier. An ASO arrangement eliminates this factor as the group bears the responsibility for incurred and unreported claims. It becomes a contingent liability only materializing in the event of a termination of a contract with a carrier where a subsequent carrier commences on a premium basis.

Since there is no insured risk, the carrier may potentially allow for more flexibility in plan design. Eligibility requirements can also be less stringent (e.g., retirees, consultants).

Disadvantages

ASO arrangements are not regulated by the Insurance Act (e.g., change of carrier, disclosure). As a result, employees are not afforded any protection as with an insured plan.

There is a possibility of underfunding the plan if the group does not maintain an appropriate level of funds to offset incurred but not reported claims in the event of termination of the ASO arrangement.

This is a very serious concern if either the long-term disability or life insurance benefits are self-insured, due to the significant liability attached to these claims and the extended duration of payment. We anticipate government regulation relative to provision of pooled benefits on an ASO basis, which, in essence, will limit the availability of this option. As a result, we would recommend insuring both of these benefits.

Without a stop-loss provision, a catastrophic loss could have a major impact on cash flow.

Certain contractual privileges normally provided under an insured plan (e.g., conversion privilege) are not available under an ASO arrangement.

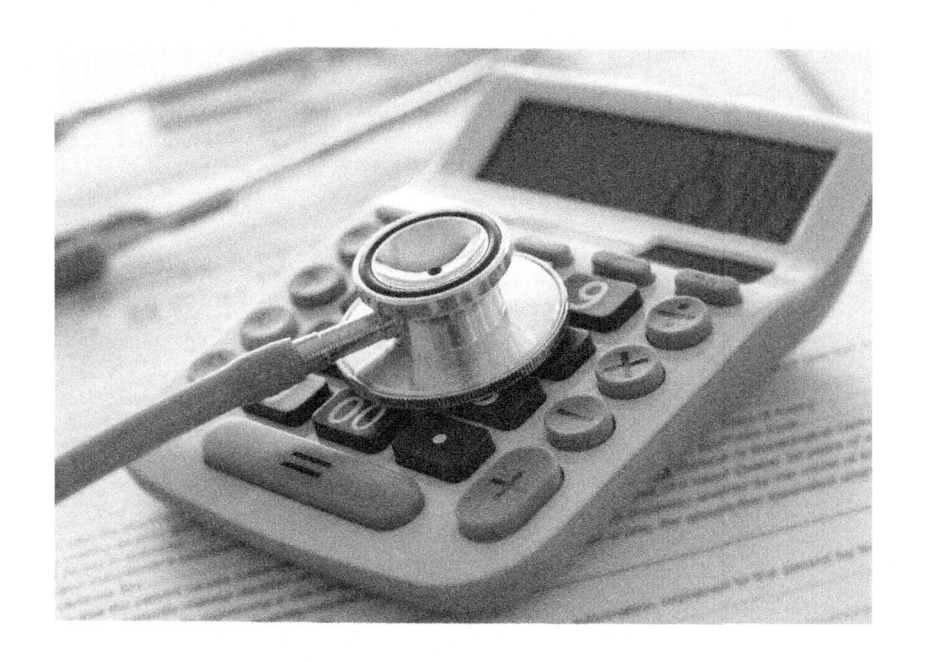

Section 7

The Pillars of Business
Who Pays the Bill

NETWORKING

Centers of Influence

> The richest people in the world look for and build networks. Everyone else looks for work.
> —Robert Kiysoaki

How true is this?

In fact, we are networking. However, in generating business leads, it's not about who you know but more about who knows you. So the question is, do the people you want to do business with know you?

Networking by its definition is about promoting pathways to success by connecting with other business people to further each other's business interest and forming mutually beneficial business relationships.

So if we can all agree, people will only do business with those they know, like and trust, why aren't more people actively networking?

Here are some facts to support more active connecting toward the common goal of surviving this economic downturn.

According to the January 8, 2016, Treasury Board and Finance report "Economics and Revenue Forecasting," Alberta lost 63,500 jobs in the first eight months of 2015, the largest since the same period in 2009. Alberta's employment declined by 3,900 in December 2015, adding to the 25,700 losses in the previous two months. Over 2015, the unemployment rate increased by 2.5 percentage points and averaged 6.0 percent for the year.

Not good news. But what that tells me is, as business owners, we've been there before, and if we pull together, as we have in the past, we will get through it this time as well.

According to *Forbes Magazine*, the best source of new business is referrals from happy clients. You cannot receive a better lead than one sent your way with a strong referral. You cannot have a more motivated prospect arrive than someone sent there by a raving fan.

The challenge is: How do you get satisfied customers to actively promote you to their social and professional networks?

Constantly ask for referrals. Do this in the midst of delivering excellent service, while still actively involved with the client. You deliver great value and want more people to benefit, so ask, "Who do you know?"

Build a centre of influence (COI) circle consisting of people happy to refer you to others.

Make sure those in your COI know what kind of businesses you're interested in servicing. If your network doesn't know what kind of clients you are interested in, you may spin your wheels on non-productive, non-money-making leads.

So practicing what I preach, if you know of any business owners in need of a strategically designed, constantly serviced, inclusive benefit plan, please send them my way.

THE CORPORATE POLICY

Protecting the Employer's Interest

Many companies overlook the necessity of a corporate policy to educate, address and, most importantly, protect the reasoning behind their decision-making process. Current employees, as well as new, should be informed as to why certain decisions are made according to company protocol. A good example of this is the extension of health and dental benefits when an employee is approved for a long-term disability claim.

The corporate policy booklet should clearly define how long health and dental benefits will be extended while an employee is on long-term disability. Otherwise there would be no end date, and the employer will be responsible for providing these benefits to the employee until their termination age according to the policy contract.

Take, for example, an employee who is 41and qualifies for long-term disability. According to most group insurance policy contracts, that employee would be eligible to receive health and dental benefits until age 70—29 years! If there is no corporate policy in place, then the company is responsible for contributing their portion to retain this coverage for the impacted employee.

How long a company will continue to offer these benefits to a disabled employee is the decision of the employer; however, once the precedence is set, it should be reviewed by legal counsel, maintained and written down for reference for all existing and new employees. A corporate policy approved by a lawyer will protect the company against expenses in continuing to supply these benefit privileges.

It is important to note that the employment standard act currently deems an employee approved for long-term disability to be the same as an employee not on a long-term disability claim.

If a corporate policy is not present to clearly define how long the company will extend the group health and dental benefits, and there is presently an employee approved for long-term disability, then the employer should be cautious on how or when to terminate benefits from the employee, which were currently provided when he or she was not on a disability claim. Without a properly written policy, there are potential legal implications because of precedent—no defined end date for coverage. Randomly electing a date to terminate could potentially be viewed as "anti-selection" or "prejudice" and is the very reason for why a corporate policy is a must. A corporate policy will ensure all employees are treated equally.

If there is already corporate policy in place, then the above becomes a non-issue for the company, the employee and the employee's dependents.

FRAUD

The Real Issue of Benefit Fraud

Benefit fraud is a real issue, and its impact is significant. By its nature, fraud is intended to be concealed, and that is precisely what makes the full impact on group benefits hard to estimate. Fraud typically occurs when opportunity (perception that there's little chance of detection, penalty or consequence), rationalization (entitlement to additional money paid out of the benefit plan) and pressure (desire for financial gain) combine.

A Canadian authority on health-care fraud in Canada—the Canadian Health Care Anti-fraud Association—estimates fraud accounts for between 2 percent to 10 percent of total health-care spending in Canada or better put, anywhere between $440 million and $2.2 billion in losses annually—losses that ultimately translate into higher premiums for plan sponsors.

From an employer's perspective, consider a plan with 100 employees and premiums between $300,000 and $400,000 per year. Fraud could represent up to $40,000 yearly. In light of benefit costs growing at or near double-digit annual rates for most of the last decade, an aging workforce and drug costs escalating, when fraud is added into the equation, within five years, costs due to fraud could grow by more than 50 percent, or $60,000 annually.

Types of Fraud

Provider fraud is when health-care service providers acts to exploit the plan for their own personal gain. This can be done by submitting false claims in the names of existing patients whereby the claims are set to pay the provider of the service. The employee doesn't even know.

Plan member fraud is when an employee acts to exploit the plan for his or her own personal gain. False invoices are submitted for treatments or equipment never received by the employee.

Providers and plan member collusion is when health-care providers and employees work together to exploit the plan for mutual gain. Consider a health-care facility collaborating with employees to submit false claims for services and products never rendered or dispensed, then splitting the funds between the provider and employees. Another example is employees receiving paramedical treatments from unregistered providers and submitting claims for medical equipment instead.

This is a growing concern due to a lack of understanding of the impact of fraud. The less informed people are, the more susceptible they are to fall victim to its impact because it's not on their radar to be aware. That being said, the insurance industry has implemented checks and balances, including random audits on prepayments, providers and web-based claims, to name a few, to stay ahead of this rising threat. These efforts have saved millions of dollars a year in claim recovery.

Technology, the Fertilizer for Benefit Fraud

Life is so much easier these days. Remember the excitement when pay direct drug cards were first introduced? How did point-of-sale claims for pharmacy and dental go from being an added perk to mainstream? Now look at the average consumer with a benefit plan. Massage therapy is directly processed, and there's an app for that if it's not—photo claims and texting ability. Easy is the name of the game.

Fraud is also a game—a game with serious consequences.

As easy as it is to make claims and be reimbursed in minutes, it adds a spark to fuel the fire of abuse of the system and then on to fraud.

Abuse and fraud don't just cost the insurer of the benefit. They cost the employer and, ultimately, the end users, the employees, through increased rates and perhaps reduced access to care required. The Canadian Health Care Fraud Survey suggests about 95 percent of Canadian benefit plans have been victimized by fraudulent claims, representing 2 to 10 percent of claims. To put this in perspective, millions, perhaps billions of dollars are spent each year. Now the math of fraud becomes clearer.

The most common types of benefits fraud among employees are submitting false claims for services they didn't receive and increasing the number or dollar amount of services provided. While technology makes it easier to manufacture fraudulent claims, it also provides the means to better track, analyze and, ultimately, trace patterns of abuse of the system.

Pattern-recognition technology allows insurers to estimate a particular provider's revenue or capacity and put an algorithm in place to identify the trend line for that provider. When claim patterns move off that trend line, it triggers an investigation.

While employee fraud is a concern, actual provider fraud is the bigger problem, representing about 87 percent of fraudulent activity. Consider a recent client experience where the owner's wife goes to fill a prescription. The plan is set at 100 percent, yet she was charged an additional $7.34. The pharmacist suggested her plan was not accurately set up to pay the claim, suggesting the claim would only cover generic and the drug was brand name. This was not the case at all.

Fortunately, she was well aware of the plan parameters and knew the plan was set to cover as submitted, including brand-name drugs. This additional money went over and above the dispensing fee, the reasonable and customary limits and in the end because of the early intervention, the additional funds were refunded and the customer took her business elsewhere.

But this is a concern. Some may look at this example and say, "Seven dollars and thirty-four cents? Big deal." That's 3 percent of the claim cost, and if that type of procedure is in place for all claims going through that pharmacy, consider the amounts daily, weekly and yearly—staggering.

This is an example of billing for services not rendered. Others to be aware of are claiming a more expensive procedure than what was actually done, treating outside of one's scope of practice and using unlicensed people to treat but billing said treatment through someone else's license number.

Because of our socialized system of health care, where the private plan supplements the government offering, often there's a sense of entitlement around benefits that help people rationalize their actions. For that reason, employers need to change how they think about and communicate the necessity for everyone to be on board to spot fraud as it happens. The best protection is awareness and early intervention. If rates are escalating due to high claims activities, investigate those sudden spikes in claims. Are the legitimate?

Remember, these dollars belong to you.

Missing the Shoe Box

Technology—love it! Can't live without it. But sometimes, I shake my head and wonder if I'm better off without all of these "advancements"—applications, ease of use systems and streamlined access.

Consider that we are only a couple of decades into point-of-sale drug cards and claim submission from the dentist direct to the insurer. Gone are the days of the shoe box and saving up claims for bulk submission for reimbursement. Don't get me wrong: these advancements are all good. Online and smartphone services save the consumer—the employee—time, energy, effort and, a lot of times, frustration. The acceleration of claims processing and reimbursement means a claim submitted digitally today can be in the employee's bank account tomorrow. Wow. That's fast.

But there's a cost to the digital age.

The speed of technological advancement has also created an increased claiming opportunity. There is no missed opportunity—nothing left in the shoe box. There is an attitude of entitlement from plan members that everything should be claimable, while at the same time, consumers have lost a fundamental appreciation for just how much is spent on benefits—perhaps billions of dollars each year in Canada—because they are not paying out of pocket for it first. The direct claim submission has meant a reduced awareness of the actual costs and amount of claiming activity.

Consider how many times I facilitate an employee meeting where the number-one rebuke to rate hikes is "I don't use the plan." Yes, they went to the dentist twice that year, as did the spouse and children. A few prescriptions, vision and let's not forget the occasional massage, yet because everything was direct processing, the perception of actual claim activity diminished. What likely amounted to between $3,000 and $4,000 in claims had the perception of a couple of hundred dollars because that was all they were out of pocket due to coinsurance. Because there is no little out-of-pocket expense, no one can blame the average employee for this perception. Yet these false perceptions—the lack of awareness of claim activity—devalues the benefit plan overall.

It's true, digital innovations are transforming health care, with huge implications for benefit plan sponsors and the employees they serve. There are estimated to be between eight hundred and one thousand health care–related technology start-ups in Canada today.

The big question is how do employers create an awareness of the plan's value, while maintaining the ease with which employees have come to appreciate their claims being reimbursed?

Always open to suggestions.

ICE CREAM

The Customer Service Advantage

> "I like how you break things down. Very sensible. Thanks for all your help."
> Could there be a better compliment?
> No.

In life, though, I am a consumer like the rest of the population, so I want to be treated in the same manner I treat my clients—like they are the only client in the world to me. It happens, but more infrequently than I would like.

Case in point, I like ice cream. I am a little kid at heart in that respect, and there is nothing like a nice evening out with the family and an ice cream cone to widen the smile.

So there we are at our favorite ice cream shop, a major chain with no real competition in the marketplace, and the people behind the counter (not the teens everyone expects to blame this on but people old enough to know better) are slouching, sloppy, leaning on the counter and generally uninterested in the job at hand. We received no focus, no attention to detail and no thank-you for spending the premium prices charged for iced milk.

The order is placed, and we are waiting. And we wait. The shop is not busy, and there is a general feeling of inactivity. A singing employee in the back is putting burgers together with ninja chops, complete with sound effects (you think I am putting on, and I am not!). There is the whippersnapper dish-towel-flinging cashier, and I wonder how any orders are being filled.

Other than the drive-through, there are hardly any orders, and I'm beginning to see why the large restaurant is almost empty.

Our order for a family of four, just on ice cream, covered the salary of one of the eight employees I counted inside for at least an hour and a half, so there is no question there was enough money coming in the door. So can no one take the time to ensure these representatives of the company platform stand up straight, take pride in their job and get the work done the way it is supposed to get done to the best quality available? Or is it just that they really have no competition for their product and, hence, no real need to treat the customer better? Could it be we are all just so used to buying our ice cream there that we don't even think about going anywhere else?

This type of attitude transfers over, I realize, into a lot of areas where we spend money. As creatures of habit, we are used to buying our groceries at one location and our gas at another, so when the service slides, do we notice? Maybe, and then we just continue on. But what if consumers were to try something different and test the waters to see what a difference service makes to our overall enjoyment of the product?

When looking at your benefit plan and all the options provided for the employees, what would it hurt to test the waters? Do you see the differences some innovation, attention to detail and grateful recipients of your business add to the overall experience?

I have to say, my ice cream would have tasted a whole lot better going down had it been given with a smile!

PROSPECTING TO CLOSE

If You're in Business, You're in Sales

Basically, if you're earning a living, you're in sales.

Whether you use these skills to close the sale, get a loan at the bank, hire skilled staff members or get services and supplies to increase business productivity, essential sales skills are mandatory to performance.

Contrary to popular belief, closing a sale is only the first step to increasing your sales, not the last. After-sale service shows customers you want to build a long-term relationship, earn their loyalty and keep their business. This will in turn encourage current customers to refer business to others. At the end of the day, you will increase sales and profitability over the long term.

There are no quick fixes. Achieving good sales skills takes time, and after-sales service, for me, includes living by what was promised at the onset—the reason the customer decided to spend his or her hard-earned dollars with MP benefits over the competition. This also includes following up, offering ongoing education and, most importantly, effectively dealing with complaints and concerns from both the claiming process and administrative delivery from the insurance provider.

Recognize that we live in a world of constant change. Whatever product we sell or deliver is a victim of this change. To effectively service clients, it is important they hear about industry changes and innovations from us and not the competition. The quickest way to lose a client is to not keep them up to date, not to mention the missed opportunity.

It's true, not everyone will necessarily want to make these changes. They are happy and satisfied with the status quo, but by keeping clients up-to-date, you've given them a chance to be educated and offered another opportunity to share the messaging with others who may in fact be interested. This is an essential element in the trust economy, which stretches further than any other currency.

Sometimes going the extra mile pays off with dividends. When there is an opportunity to use knowhow to assist in a troubleshooting exercise, which would typically not fall within the realm of the product offering, this will be deed not soon forgotten.

And never forget the power of thank you. Use all available interactions to make sure the customer feels valued. Establish a rapport. It's true, I'm proud to say, that many clients have become friends.

Information is key.

- Clarify what the client is buying, and always give them a way out.
- Explain the process to satisfy complaints.
- Be enthusiastic about what you sell.
- Provide updates on the latest information—always.
- Invite customer feedback—keep in touch and connect.
- Provide innovative changes as they happen. Don't wait to be asked.
- Get personal. Get to know the customer's businesses to refer them.
- Encourage clients to ask questions. Let them know they can trust that even if you don't know the answer, you will find someone who can help.
- If you can't help, find someone who can and get back to clients with a referral or suggestion.
- Show examples where the latest innovations may work for them in the future—if not at the present.
- Follow up on any queries, ensuring the situation has been resolved.
- The Golden Rule: Be generous with your time; give the personal attention you would like to receive.

INCOME TAX ACT

Employee Benefit Plan Taxation

Who Is Taxed?

The three parties concerned with the tax consequences of benefits resulting from employment, including benefits negotiated under collective agreements, are:

1. The employee, who is primarily concerned with whether the benefit or the contribution for the benefit is taxable to him or her or exempt from tax and in contributory plans, whether employee contributions are deductible from income
2. The employer, who is primarily concerned with the deductibility of any contributions toward employee benefits from its income and the timing of such deduction
3. The trust fund, subject to certain exceptions, is a taxable entity to the extent that it earns any investment income, subject to deductions from income pertaining to expenditures required to earn such income, to administer the trust and certain taxable payments to beneficiaries. Accordingly, interest or dividend income earned by a trust fund, as a result of trustees' obligation to make the trust assets productive, may result in some income tax consequences unless proper tax-planning measures are undertaken.

What Is Taxed?

The Income Tax Act purports to tax income. This concept of income has historically proven to be very difficult to define and has generated much debate among experts in the field. Problems as to what is deductible from income have compounded the issues even further.

In the case of employee benefits, determining what is income is not particularly difficult. Employee income is the remuneration paid to an employee over the course of a taxation year in money or its equivalent arising from the employment of such employee, subject to certain deductions, exemptions and tax credits.

An employer's income is its net income as a result of carrying on business, subject to the deductibility of costs of doing business, including benefit costs.

As for the trust fund itself, its income is generally derived from interest, dividends and capital gains, less certain deductions that are reviewed below.

It is important to note that there are a number of employee benefits that, although they would otherwise constitute income, are exempt from taxation pursuant to specific provisions of the Income Tax Act, which we review below. Further, certain types of trust funds are exempt from taxation on their income.

Taxation of Employee Income Section 5 of the Income Tax Act is the general taxing provision regarding income from office or employment. It states, "Subject to this Part, a taxpayer's income for a taxation year from an office or employment is the salary, wages and other remuneration, including gratuities, received by him in the year."

Section 5 takes a broad view of income and remuneration and seeks to include virtually any benefit. To the extent that section 5 is not explicit, section 6(1)(a) of the act specifies that there shall be included in computing the income of a taxpayer for a taxation year as income from an office or employment, "the value of board, lodging and other benefits of any kind whatever received or enjoyed by him in the year in respect of, in the course of, or by virtue of an office or employment," subject to certain exceptions. Accordingly, the act specifies that any remuneration from employment or any benefits whatsoever is taxable unless one can find a specific exemption for the benefit in the act.

Section 6(1)(a)(i) of the act specifically exempts from tax the value of benefits derived from an employer's contributions to or under a registered pension plan, group sickness or accident insurance plan, private health services plan, supplementary unemployment benefit plan, deferred profit-sharing plan or group term life insurance policy. As a consequence, an employer's contributions to a fund in respect of any of these plans do not trigger any tax consequences for employee beneficiaries of that fund unless other provisions of the Income Tax Act bring the contributions back into taxable income.

The receipt of certain benefits by an employee from a fund or from the insurer with which that fund contracts may, however, trigger tax consequences for the employee. For example, section 6(1)(f) of the act provides that the following amounts are included in an employee's income:

> 6(1)(f) the aggregate of amounts received by him in the year that were payable to him on a periodic basis in respect of the loss of all or any part of his income from an office or employment, pursuant to:
> i. sickness or accident insurance plan, or
> ii. disability insurance plan, or
> iii. an income maintenance insurance plan to or under which his employer has made a contribution.

On the other hand, an employee's receipt of benefits exempt from tax pursuant to section 6(1)(a) and not taxable pursuant to other sections of the act remain non-taxable. Thus, benefits provided to an employee under a private health services plan, such as drug, medical and supplementary health benefits, are not subject to tax. As well, lump-sum payments to an employee's estate or a named beneficiary as a result of a group term life insurance policy are not taxable in the recipient's hands.

Employer Deductibility

The act requires, under section 18(1), that no taxpayer make deductions from income from a business or property, unless such outlay or expense "was made or incurred by the taxpayer for the purpose of gaining or producing income from the business or property."

Payments mandated under a collective agreement are payments of labor costs for purposes of gaining or producing income and are deductible by the employer. There are, of course, limitations on such deductions, to the extent that contributions for certain types of benefits are involved. There are special limitations for:

1. Supplementary unemployment benefit plans
2. Registered pension plan contributions
3. Employee benefit plan contributions
4. Contributions to employee trusts
5. Contributions to retirement compensation arrangements.

In discussing the taxation of the specific benefits below, we will deal with the concept of employer deductibility in each case. Expenses for benefit costs are generally deductible from employer income in the year in which they are incurred. However, in respect of contributions to an employee benefit plan, there is no employer deduction until the year in which the employee receives the benefits, subject to certain adjustments set out in sections 18 and 32.1 of the act.

Taxation of Trusts

Trusts are separate legal entities and are taxable on their income. The trust is the most common method of holding plan assets for multiemployer plans established under collective agreements. Certain individuals are generally named as trustees, and they are responsible for the obligations of the fund, including the payment of any taxes. The taxation of trusts is a complex and difficult area, particularly when dealing with testamentary and charitable trusts. Trusts established for the purpose of providing employee benefits are subject to the general rules for the taxation of trusts, with certain exceptions set out in the act itself or in Revenue Canada Interpretation Bulletins. In general, there are three categories of trusts:

1. Trusts that are totally tax exempt on their income, such as registered pension plans, group retirement savings plans, supplementary unemployment benefit plans and certain qualifying vacation pay trust funds
2. Trust funds subject to special rules, such as health and welfare trusts covered by Interpretation Bulletin IT-85R21 or employee benefit plans and employee trusts covered by Interpretation Bulletin IT-502
3. All other trusts that are subject to the general rules for taxation of trusts

With respect to the general rules of taxation of trusts, section 104(2) of the act taxes a trust as if it were an individual. Generally, trusts are taxed at the highest personal rate in Canada, and accordingly, it is important to attempt to avoid taxation of any income of a trust, if at all possible.

Trusts can deduct certain expenses from their gross income, namely the following:

- Expenses incurred in earning the income and certain administrative expenses of operating the trust
- Money paid or payable directly to beneficiaries of the trust during any tax year (subject to certain limitations set out in section 104(6) of the Act for employee benefit plans and employee trusts), which is then taxed in the hands of the beneficiary

As a general proposition, the costs of providing nontaxable premiums and benefits payable to employees out of the trust fund are not deductible from the income of the trust. Revenue Canada has also adopted a policy in respect of taxable multiemployer plan trusts, to the effect that any trust with gross income in excess of $500 must file a T3 income tax return (see IT-85R2 and IT-502).

Employee Benefit Plans and Employee Trusts

Employee benefits not paid directly by the employer to its employees may be delivered in three different ways, each of which has distinct tax implications. One vehicle for delivering benefits is the health and welfare trust, which may provide those health and welfare benefits set out in section 6(1)(a)(i) of the Income Tax Act. (Health and welfare trusts are considered in section 3.) The second and third vehicles are the employee benefit plan and the employee trust. Each of these arrangements involves a third-party custodian in the administration of the benefit plan.

Employee Benefit Plans

An employee benefit plan is generally defined in section 248 of the Income Tax Act as any arrangement under which an employer makes contributions to another person (the custodian) and under which payments are made to or for the benefit of employees or former employees. An arrangement that provides only for benefits that are expressly excluded from income by reason of subparagraph 6(1)(a)(i) of the act is not an employee benefit plan but may be a health and welfare trust. As well, section 248 specifically excludes certain other plans, such as employee trusts, vacation pay trusts, education and training arrangements, retirement compensation arrangements and prescribed plans from employee benefit plan status.

The tax treatment of employees, employers and custodians involved in an employee benefit plan is somewhat complex. Under subsection 6(1)(g) of the Income Tax Act, an employee is required to take into his or her income the value of taxable benefits received from the employee benefit plan in the year in which such benefits are received. It is noteworthy that all amounts taxable under subsection 6(1)(g) are fully taxable as income from employment, regardless of how the plan received its income (as employer contributions, capital gains, dividends, etc.) and regardless of the fact that such income previously may have been taxed in the custodian's hands.

If it is organized as a trust, the employee benefit plan is taxable as a trust on its income determined under part 1 of the Income Tax Act. Contributions are not included in gross income, and payments out of those contributions or prior year's accumulated income are not deductible by the trust. The trust may deduct expenses incurred by it in earning investment income, normal operating expenses or amounts paid to beneficiaries out of the trust's current income and taxable to the beneficiaries. Where the plan is not a trust, the custodian is taxable on the plan's net income at the custodian's applicable tax rate.

The taxation rules applicable to an employer that contributes to an employee benefit plan are particularly complex. The thrust of the act's employee benefit plan provisions is to synchronize the employer's deduction of contributions with the taxation of employees who receive benefits from the plan. The mechanical complexity of this matching is most evident in the calculation of the contributing employer's tax position. Since the deductibility of the employer's contributions to an employee benefit plan is contingent on the taxation of the corresponding benefit, a contributing employer may not deduct its contribution in the year it is made but may only deduct its contribution pursuant to section 32.1 in the year it is paid out as a benefit.

The amount of the employer's deduction for a taxation year is the amount allocated under subsection 32.1(2) to the employer for that year by the plan custodian. Under subsection 32.1(2), benefits paid out of the plan are considered to come from the following:

1. The plan beneficiary contributions
2. The income of the plan for the year
3. Employer contributions
4. The plan's prior year's income, if any

Employee Trusts

An employee trust is defined in section 248 of the Income Tax Act as an arrangement whereby an employer makes contributions to a trust for the sole benefit of its employees. The employee's right to benefits must vest when the contribution is made, and the amount of the employee's benefit cannot be contingent on the employee's position, performance or compensation as an employee.

The definition of an employee trust requires that the trustee must elect that the trust be treated as an employee trust within 90 days of the end of the trust's first taxation year.

The act permits employers to deduct their contributions to employee trusts in the year in which such contributions are made. Thus, unlike employee benefit plans, the employer can deduct its contribution to the employee trust immediately and need not wait for its contribution to be paid out to the trust's beneficiaries as a benefit.

The employee trust must then allocate to its beneficiaries all employer contributions and investment income in the year in which it receives such contributions and income. The employee trust is not taxable on the income it allocates. Such allocation need not correspond with the actual payment of benefits.

Beneficiaries are taxable on such amounts as are allocated to them by the trustee in the year. The amount that is taxable to the employee in the year is not the amount of benefits actually received by the employee but rather, the amount allocated to the employee. As well, all amounts allocated by the trust to the employee are included in the employee's income, regardless of whether the trust earned any amount as capital gains or dividends.

An employee trust arrangement allows a plan to distribute the tax burden of its benefits across the entire class of its beneficiaries. Employees each pay tax on their allocated amounts, not on the value of the benefit that they may actually receive in any particular year. This type of arrangement may be particularly convenient in the case of a prepaid legal plan, for instance, where an employee's receipt of benefits could otherwise trigger a large tax liability.

Endnotes
1. Revenue Canada, Interpretation Bulletin IT-85R2, "Health and Welfare Trusts for Employees" (31 July 1986).
2. Revenue Canada, Interpretation Bulletin IT-502, "Employee Benefit Plans and Employee Trusts" (28 March 1985).

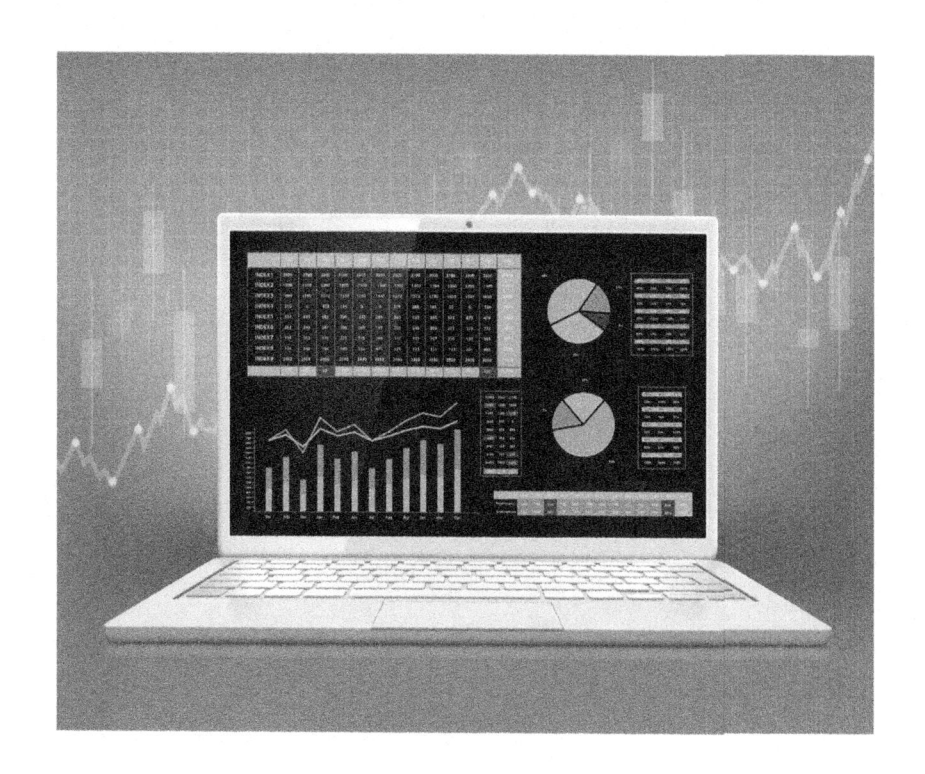

Section 8

Why Use a Broker?
Working with an Expert

WHY USE A BROKER?

The Advantage of a Specialist

Like any consumer-driven product, price is a key component to the ultimate decision to buy. When a company decides to look into benefits, they designate someone to shop—call various insured underwriters for pricing options based on their plan stipulations.

The stumbling block encountered at this stage is that most insurance underwriters do not deal directly with the client. They work through a network of brokers. This tends to frustrate the consumer, who is only seeking pricing and not yet ready to make a decision to work with one key individual.

Once consumers understand they have to work through a broker, they may typically contact two or more to interview before they decide which broker they want to work with. Most times they will want to see what kind of pricing this person can pull in before they make their decision.

Oops, stalled at the door. An insurance carrier will only release one quote to one broker. The decision has to be made prior to pricing.

Now add another layer of decision to an already frustrated client, who still simply wants pricing for a benefit plan. The perception at this point becomes, "Insurance is too complicated. There are so many rules. It is not worth my time." And they give up.

Are we losing sight of the objective or simply not aware of the process?

Step 1: Find a credible benefit broker. This professional listens and works with the client to ascertain what kind of benefits he or she is looking for—analyze their needs and address cost measures.

Step 2: After an analysis of the desired plan, the professional will contact various insurance underwriters to gather quotations for the client based upon the desired plan design that will best suit the client's unique needs.

Insurance brokers are not bound by any one insurance company. They are independent and work for the client—always. An insurance agent, on the other hand, is bound to one insurance company and works for that company only.

Step 3: Develop a plan proposal, which includes a plan design reflective of items of key importance to the employer and ultimately the plan members as a reflection of business plan and compensation. The costs associated with each of the providers for the options available and how that may be split between the owner and the employees is vital to these metrics.

Step 4: Once the benefit plan is in place, a broker will ensure it is reviewed regularly, especially as the business grows and changes, so it continues to meet the objectives of attraction and retention for employees per the overall business strategy.

Insurance can be complicated, but it doesn't have to be. We like simple, straightforward solutions that work for our clients in attaining their benefit goals.

CLIENT CENTRIC

Have you ever looked at something for a long time and then blinked, and everything looked different?

Two ears and one mouth—time to listen.

There are wants, and there are needs. Going into a breakfast meeting, people have expectations of choices of hot and cold food, and they expect the food will be tasty, satisfy hunger and provide needed energy for the start of the day. There is an expectation that the people interacting will be positive and business focused. The agenda items will be cleared, and all will move forward with their goals.

However, going into this breakfast meeting, we don't think about the needs. There is the assumption that the food will be healthy and good to eat and that we won't come away with food poisoning. We would assume the people attending want to carry on business, and we won't have an altercation or a setback.

Utilizing a client-centric formula, our goal transforms from selling a product to establishing a solution.

By establishing a partnership with customers, to understand their business, business practices, employee base and goals, we ensure decisions regarding the benefit plan reflect the wants, needs and, more importantly, preferences. This is achieved through ongoing service, communication and education.

Promoting pillars of business for the business owner and understanding the more specialized services rendered for all of their needs will ensure sound practices and successful outcomes for both the business and all who support the business. Connectivity is crucial to anyone's success, and establishing trust is paramount to this end. Therefore, our centres of influence have to be those professionals who have set themselves apart as leaders in their chosen professions and can offer our customers quality services when they need them.

Our role is work with the customer, not to focus on selling a product. This means the information and interactions and ultimately the plan design for the benefit package emanates from the client, who knows and understands their employees' needs and wants. Everything we do as brokers is built on the premise that personalized service and interactions are prompted by the customer and their employees. This then results in a benefit plan as unique as the organization itself, setting it apart in the marketplace as *the* place to work and engage and, of course, succeed.

While these ideas are not new or secret, they are still seldom focused into action in an industry still focused on the product. Being client centric every day, as brokers, involves thought and workflow processes customized to each customer, resulting in satisfied clients over the long term.

FROM GOOD TO GREAT

Benefits to Attract and Retain Employees

Good benefits are a factor of remunerations employees have come to expect in any organization worth their consideration for employment. Great benefits are options and choice components, which actually make an impact on employees' perspective of where they work and what kind of employer they have.

In today's diverse and fluctuating economy, businesses of all sizes and in all markets have come to recognize their most valuable assets to be their employees and the tax effectiveness of the employee group benefit plan. Many companies distinguish themselves by fostering strong relationships, engaging employees at the individual level and looking out for the employees' personal needs as ways to attract and preserve high-caliber people in their organizations.

Employees know they are a valuable asset to a business and how that value increases the longer they stay. As the economy begins to pick up, so will competitive job offers to tempt employees away. More than position itself, many factors influence a worker's decision to stay or move on.

With a focus on family and well-being, many consider the impacts of total compensation as key factors in whether or not to stay. Compensation includes not only wages or salary but also what the company can offer in benefits, vacation and lifestyle perquisites, such as flexible hours, accommodation of family needs and so on.

With employee benefits, companies are looking for the most cost-effective solutions to provide the coverage their workers want. One great way to offer employees cost-effective, comprehensive benefits is to top up with a health spending account.

What's a Health Spending Account (HSA)?

There is not a plan out there that can meet everyone's expectations of a benefit plan, but with a well-designed health spending account, employers not only provide more benefits for employees but also provide the most important thing for these savvy shoppers—choice in care and provider services, as well as control over how they spend their money for these services.

Unlike a more traditional style of plan, a HSA is not an insurance product. HSAs are fully funded by the employer and administered by a benefits provider to the overall set maximum.

Without question, HSAs are cost effective, with no sign-up fees, no transaction fees and no medical questionnaires to answer. The administrative fee is applied on claims only.

While HSAs are designed to suit the needs of employees and their families, they also provide tax advantages for employers and employees alike. The employee receives the compensation on claims tax free, and the employer receives a corporate tax deduction for the premium, plus the administration fees to provide the coverage.

Always check with your accountant for tax advice.

SAY WHAT YOU MEAN

Mean What You Say

Yes, advertising still exists on the radio. And I'm listening because the excellent narrator with the spot-on western twang says, "We say it. We mean it. And more importantly, we do it."

And I'm hooked.

In a world full of social and mass media, loads of companies "say it," and obviously they "mean it" or why bother; but it wasn't the "we do it" that grabbed me. It was the "more importantly" part of his slogan, because he is right. It is one thing to say it, but it is much more important to do it.

Said another way, you can put the worm on the hook to bait the fish, and you can catch the fish, but can you prepare the fish in a meal that is both edible and likable? That truly is the challenge.

As benefit specialist, when we say, "Proud providers of affordable employee group benefits," you know what? We mean it! *Affordable* doesn't mean *cheap*. *Affordable* means working within the client's budget to establish and create a plan that works over the long term. We consistently (yet another great word with meaning) provide savings for our clients. We do this through custom-designed solutions combined with consistent service standards, treating every client as though he or she were our only client.

These are not just words that sound good; these are words with meaning.

Our plans follow the KIS (keep it simple) approach, and many accuse us initially of being too easy because consumers have been conditioned to accept complicated situations in the benefits world, but broken down, benefits are not complicated, nor do they have to be.

We build to suit. Listening to clients means providing benefits to fit their needs, because let's not forget: each company's benefit plan is as unique as a fingerprint and should be treated as such.

Are you unique?

Of course you are!

Don't you deserve a benefit package that is as unique as your business approach?

We really do mean what we say!

STRATEGIES EQUALS SOLUTIONS

Building Relationships

"[Our] objective is not to close the sale, but to open a relationship."

When it is necessary, perhaps because the client has no existing benefits in place, we must offer a market summary. When the customer has an existing benefit plan, an analysis is the first step to understanding why they have invited a new broker to the table.

In preparing a proposal for group insurance, the following information is necessary:

a) current employee census data
b) an apples-to-apples comparison of the current plan arrangement (if there is a plan in place)
c) an apples-to-oranges comparison based on plan design strategies, where the client wants the plan to go based on future goals for compensation and business plan
d) an accurate assessment based upon current rates and previous experience history
e) suggestions for improvement

For the existing client, the following services are provided on an ongoing basis:

a) assistance in claims
b) education and training of the plan administrator
c) employee meetings
d) information resources necessary to properly maintain the benefit plan

e) experience reporting, premiums paid, versus claims from plan members
f) pillars of business seminars for employees and plan administrators
g) newsletters, blogs and links specific to current and emerging trends
h) business owner updates on information that affects their bottom line

The renewal process includes the following:

a) an analysis of plan usage and proposed rates
b) Does the plan still meet the corporate strategies?
c) a look at future tactics
d) attention to the details that enhance employee appreciation of the plan
e) current coverage options
f) a review of the marketplace standards

LISTENING TO UNDERSTAND

Getting What You Want

Back-to-school time means, among other things, new shoes for the kids in my house—two pairs, one for inside and one for out on the playground. I head out to the mall in September and ask the sales clerk for a shoe my son likes in size four and a half, please. She comes back and earnestly tells me she has a size three and a size ten.

I think, *Um, okay, what part of the request didn't she understand?*

If he has a four-and-a-half-sized foot, it is unlikely I will squeeze him into a three or have him swim in a size ten. If you cannot provide me with what I have asked for, say so and send me on my way. Wasting my time does not adhere me to the business or invite me to come back in the future.

We've all been there—whether at the drive-through window, the retail outlet or the car dealership. You ask for one thing and expect to receive what you asked for, only to be disappointed when it doesn't come through.

The same is true in group benefits. If you have asked for 80 percent prescription drug coverage, for example, and told employees they have coverage for their pharmaceuticals, how disappointed are you in the process, the insurance carrier and, ultimately, the broker who sold you the plan when employees come back wondering why the prescription their doctor prescribed was not covered?

Is it because the plan only covers least cost alternative drugs? Perhaps the plan is hampered by formulary structures or new limitations imposed by the insurance provider.

You can get what you want. You don't have to accept a cookie-cutter plan for coverage. With the right benefit broker providing the most accurate information at the onset, employers get the plan they want, because ultimately, it's their money, and it should be spent wisely.

WE VERSUS THEY

Working with a Specialist

If there is a question that comes up time and time again, it is, "What is the difference between you and the other guys doing the same thing?"

For so long, benefit plans have been placed by a generalist who tells clients, "I can do that too," which has devalued the unique positioning, extra care, preferred pricing and expertise provided by a specialist.

First things first: someone might say, "I can do that too," but that does not essentially translate into fact. Offering custom-designed packages that reflect the corporation's core values takes a specific set of skills. Being able to hone relationships with underwriters to offer out-of-the-box solutions takes effort. Building benefits to include traditional insured products merged with administrative services only (ASO) options, in combination with health spending accounts (HSA), takes knowhow. Entrusting the value this brings into the workforce is a necessary part of the business plan.

Ease of claims, proper education and availability for questions to address the concerns of both staff members and administration alike require an ability to work well with the human resource strategy. The corporate lawyer, the accountant and the people surrounding and providing advice should fill that trusted position as core influencers and know how to work together for the great good of the company, all doing their part to ensure clients' success in their chosen marketplace.

Administration of claims is important. There is no need to even have a benefit plan if it is not (1) tax effective and (2) easy to use.

Claims need to be adjudicated for authenticity to ensure they are CRA compliant. There are no rubber stamps, and the privacy of the claimer is protected. Transparency is essential. An employer or an administrator can know via online reports what service category has been claimed and how much (pharmacy, health services, vision or dental) but never who has made that claim.

Online services allow administrators to add, terminate and make employee changes right in the system. These days claims can be reimbursed not within weeks or days but hours from the point of entry, as the system has the ability to put the money directly into the employee's account.

"Proudly turning benefits on its edge" is more than a tagline to us; it is a way of doing business.

WHAT ABOUT THE SERVICE

More than Just the Sale

How many times do we as consumers get excited about that big purchase, only to be let down by the lack of service after the sale? Something is lost in the value of the purchase when that happens.

It has been said that "service after the sale is where the rubber hits the road," and I believe this to be a fundamental truth.

In selling insurance, acquiring a client is simply the first step. Keeping the customer as a satisfied client, building a trusting relationship and being willing to refer our services to others are the goals. The only way to achieve this is to build a long-term rapport with each and every client by being responsive and answering questions or concerns as they happen, when it matters.

Clients have the ability to choose anyone to satisfy their financial and insurance goals. The insurance arena is a saturated market and is highly competitive. The fact that our clients have chosen us is a privilege we strive to never forget. Building their loyalty through excellent customer care to retain their business is a fundamental business goal.

In achieving this goal, we do the following:

- Provide personalized service. We know our clients by name because they mean something to us. We never want our clients to have to tell and re-tell their issue or concern to achieve a solution or remedy.
- Keep notes and follow up until the situation has been resolved.
- Ensure correct contact information to access services immediately.

- Make ourselves available to answer questions or concerns regarding claiming issues.
- Assist with form completion.
- Provide guidance when a catastrophic event occurs, such as a life, disability or critical illness.
- Assist with enrollments and terminations from the benefit plan.
- Ensure that when there are additional insured needs required, you speak to an expert.
- Make recommendations based on the most appropriate product to fill the need.
- Never allow price to influence the product recommendation.
- Research, stay informed and stay educated on the products and companies we represent.
- Respect a no answer when something does not meet the client's expectations regarding additional products or services.
- Most of all, are thankful for your business.

WHY SPECIALIZE?

Something to consider—in my professional existence, I have always been a group benefit specialist. Although I am educated in money matters, individual insurance and financial planning, that is not where I shine, and therefore, I leave those elements to those professionals who really sparkle in that capacity. I have an ongoing beef with the generalist who professes, "I can do that too." Recently, in a conversation with one such individual, I painted the following fictional picture:

> Though I have never invested money for client in the past, I have a client who is unhappy with their current adviser and asks if I can take care of their money matters for them, as they have trusted me with their benefit plan for many years, and I have never let them down. In this fictional scenario, I say, "Yes, I can do that too." Now the client entrusts their lifelong assets in my not-so-capable hands. What do I do? I call someone who may know something to direct me to the next steps and fumble around until I feel comfortable placing the client's money somewhere according to what they indicated they wanted.

Okay, I have to stop there. I'm breaking out in a sweat just thinking about it. As fundamentally wrong as that scenario sounds—and make no mistake, it is wrong—it is also a mistake to assume the investment person will be the best consultant for a benefit plan. Dealing with a jack of all trades and master of none is like endorsing the lazy man's load. Eventually, the plates will fall.

Working exclusively to provide employee group benefit programs for employers, I have chosen a profession of service. In doing what we do best, employee group benefit specialists ensure the employer's promise of a sound well-being for their employees is fulfilled and that their employees and, by contact, those employees' families are provided with the sound coverage they not only need but also deserve on a cost-effective, tax-effective basis.

Being available and able to answer and address issues of concern when they happen, as they happen without a runaround makes all the difference. This experience results in long-term success for the business, the employer and their greatest asset: their employees.

Remember, a properly designed, well-executed benefit plan protects against those catastrophic events and provides long-term cost savings.

THE BROKER

Exclusively Working with Employee Group Benefits

There is more to implementing an employee group benefit plan than price. Much like purchasing a car, you can have an old "beater" to get you from here to there. Or you can get a new vehicle to travel in luxury and style. Of course, *there* is a vague term, and a million roads can get you to the same location if you have all the time in the world. Navigating the best road is the broker's role.

What you purchase for coverage and how that coverage is delivered may be distinctly different. For instance, when you go to the pharmacy counter for a prescription, do you care if the drug is covered under the provincial or national drug formulary? Do you even know what that means? All anyone in that situation is concerned about is that the doctor has prescribed a specific medication and you need it filled—without hassle.

Every business is unique in its own right. It is this distinctiveness that deserves a customized plan strategically built especially for them? A benefit broker does not work for one particular insured underwriter. He or she works for the client. In that capacity, a benefit broker provides personalized service to advise not only on price and plan design but also on definitions of coverage and the impact of trying to use the existing coverage under those parameters.

A benefit broker who specializes in employee group benefit plans is an extended arm of the human resources team. Providing expert advice on plan design, cost and tax savings, a benefit broker is there to deliver timely information, amend the plan when required, negotiate price points and compare the benefit plan and rate structure not only across the industry in which the client operates but also across the insured benefit providers available to ensure best price point for the coverage implemented. By monitoring market conditions, this in turn will always ensure a valuable return on the investment made in the employee's well-being.

Points to consider for engaging a broker include the following:

- An agent works directly for a specific insurance underwriter with the ability to only sell that carrier's products. A broker will engage multiple insurance carriers to obtain the best coverage, rates, service and products.
- Understanding that one shoe does not fit all, an employee group benefit specialist will provide consultation on the advantages of using the best services from each available carrier to streamline a unique and valuable benefit plan for employees.
- At times, the number-one issue for a new benefit plan is trying to decide what to implement for your employees. A benefit broker will look at your industry and provide advice on what is fairly standard for your occupational category.
- Whether you decide to work directly with an insurance company or through a broker, the same commissions are paid either way. Business owners have to decide what the best use of their money is—to pay for additional services and objective expertise or to give that extra money to the insurance carrier with no extras involved.

Now the question is this: Why wouldn't you engage a quality broker?

COMPLAINTS HAPPEN

Issues, questions, concerns—they're all part of the job description.

Hey, it's an employee group benefit plan—a group of differing insured products, grouped together for a group of distinct individuals, grouped together through common employment. Therein lies the recipe for, "You can't please everyone all the time."

But you try.

Part of what makes a broker stand out in a saturated community like insurance is that the broker works for the client, not the insurance carrier. And for that reason, when the customer is dissatisfied, it is imperative to respond. A lost client is lost revenue, and therefore, every customer should be treated as though he or she is the only client who matters.

Upset customers come in all states and phases—from not having a claim paid correctly, to errors on dates of birth, family members not added, late applicants, employees not wanting to participate, overdue bills, incorrect billing statements, to when to use technology, to name a few. The challenge is always to handle each situation as it arises in a timely fashion, in a way that leaves the customer feeling appreciated, that his or her complaint was valid and received the attention it deserved to come to a reasonable remedy.

When it comes down to it, many customers don't even bother to complain. They simply leave when the next broker walks through the door. Research suggests that up to 80 percent of customers who leave were, in fact, satisfied with the original provider. Obviously, client satisfaction is not enough. To build loyalty, brokers today have to go above and beyond to ensure customers know and understand they are valued.

Because fire prevention (dealing with customer issues, questions and concerns) forms so much of the day-to-day, here are some of the ways we work with our clients to ensure their situation is properly dealt with to a satisfactory end.

1. First, we listen carefully to get the full story. Sometimes this means the client has to vent a little bit of previous frustrations. We understand we are simply one element of a full day, and every other encounter has coloured their perception of how their complaint will be received. Patience is key. And the complaint is seldom, if ever, personal, so there is no need to get defensive. We take notes, repeat back what we have heard, make corrections to our notes and confirm what we have heard. This shows we have listened.
2. Then we ask questions. These questions will be based on the experience of working through similar such circumstances. The more information we gather, the better we understand the perspective and are more equipped to take up the reins and get the issues resolved. We reconfirm what we know, put it together with the new information and build the criteria to take the issue further to resolution.
3. We are people too. We have problems, questions or concerns. We too hate to spend money where it seems unappreciated, so we always put ourselves in our customer's shoes. As the benefit broker, the goal is to solve the problem, not argue. We represent our client, and it is therefore important that our customers feel we are on their side and we empathize with the situation.
4. Always, it is important to apologize. As the broker, we may or may not be at fault, but that is not a concern. The fact is, we steered the client toward whatever product or service is causing an issue, and for that, we apologize that the plan is not running as smoothly as they would like. But we are here to help without blame. In this way, our goal is to diffuse the situation to move forward to satisfaction.
5. If it is not readily clear, as in the case of missed dependent information or an error on the billing statement, it is important to

ask the client what he or she expects to come from the situation. What would be an acceptable solution? Positioning ourselves as partners in business success allows us to be willing participants in solving the problem.
6. Then we work to resolution. Either the problem is solved right then and there, or we find someone who can solve it—quickly! Unfortunately, though, it may be beyond the broker's control. Sometimes we have to wait for answers from the insurance carriers or benefit providers, and research indicates that when complaints are not solved immediately and moved up the chain of command, they add to the customer's frustration. Our goal is to ensure that proper dialogue and communication continue during this process so the customer remains informed up to and including the time of resolution.

There is no getting around customer complaints, especially in employee group benefits. However, by employing these steps and taking the time to review the issues, we strive to turn challenges into something constructive and proactive.

WHERE'S THE LATHER?

Imagine you are wherever you purchase toiletries. In the aisles there are rows upon rows of shampoos. Every make is available. Prices vary. Color and bottle configuration help to market and catch the buyer's eye. How do consumers decide? And once they decide, what creates the loyalty that that is now the only brand for them?

If the choice was only based on getting hair clean, the same bar of soap we use at the kitchen sink would suffice, and the cost would be minimal. But that's not the only choice or consideration. Above price and function stand a whole set of perceived values that the product must meet to garner long-term loyalty. Does the product lather big, foamy suds? How we want our hair to feel after it's been cleaned by this shampoo matters. If there's buildup or residue, this mean a product shift—no matter the cost.

The same can be said of choosing a benefit broker to represent and build your benefit plan. On the shelf, insurance is a saturated marketplace with a multitude of professional vying for your business. What sets one apart from the other really comes down to the lather—the value added. What happens after the sale?

If the broker only got the business by promising the cheapest rates available, then all you have at the end of the day is the bar of soap at the kitchen counter. Sure, it gets the job done, but it's the bare minimum.

Then there's the broker or consultant who works with the business, listening to the needs of the employer. This broker understands the expectation of what the products need to achieve to be functional and appreciated by the workforce. Then and only then does the broker build a benefit plan designed to match these needs and wants.

Long-term loyalty in insurance is not purchased—it's earned. And it's earned by understanding lather is not a natural component in shampoo. It's added to enhance the process and create an enjoyment of the process.

OWNING THE PROFESSION

Success versus Mastery

If success is the fruition of reaching one's goals and the recognition of completion, mastery is the passionate understanding that one's goals are never complete and achieving success once is only the beginning.

I'm lucky to work with hundreds of passionate people who have taken their initial success and transformed this into masterful businesses. From roofers to plumbers, lawyers, accountants, dentists, health professionals, welders and machinists, in the oil patch and the high-rises, these people not only know what it takes to weather the storm but also are prepared to continue to face whatever comes their way, rejoicing in the good times and leading through the bad.

From them, I have learned to strive to be the best every day—don't skirt the problem, for therein lies an opportunity to improve.

Minor successes never come without a lot of tumbles, but I have learned it's not how many times you fall but how you get back up. Mistakes are made, and we must own these mistakes and move forward in the most positive light. Instead of pointing a finger as to all the reasons something didn't work, I have learned from clients to look within for those required resources to pick up and start fresh and aim for that one daily success.

In order to create a lasting impact, we must strive each and every day to do the very best job possible—to passionately complete the task, however menial, at hand. And in doing this, we will look back and realize we have become the best at what we do, masters, experts, if you will, of our chosen domain, hitting the mark not just once but constantly and consistently, day after day.

On this day of thanksgiving, I thank you—my customers for the inspiration.

WE DON'T SELL

We Solve; We Support

Salesmen aren't what they used to be.

At one point in time, a salesman's sole job was to sell or promote commercial products either in a store or visiting locations to get orders. Typically, once the purchase was made, you never saw or heard from that salesman again. The door-to-door peddler comes to mind or the used car dealer—someone known for his or her ability to fast-talk a customer and close the deal.

But with the age of the Internet and vast expanses of information available globally—everyone connected through some form of social media platform—those days are, fortunately, all but over.

By today's standards, by the time we walk on the car lot—if, in fact, we do walk onto the lot in person, rather than virtually—we have already checked numerous consumer guides, participated in chat rooms and spoken socially through many networks to gather opinions. So walking onto that lot has morphed into not what you can "sell" me, because I've already decided to buy, but what I am getting over and above the car I'm purchasing.

Today, insurance brokers don't "sell" employee group benefits. This is not a commodity to be traded back and forth. Benefit brokers must offer customers the opportunity to work with someone who will cut through the jargon and communicate both to their management team and the employees what they are getting, how best to access their plan and make claims and whom to call when things don't go the way they thought it would.

The benefit broker is now the consultant, the trusted adviser, the relationship partner tasked with solving problems—someone able to view the corporation through the eyes of the employer, someone who understands issues happen and real-time thinking is imperative to long-term solutions, hence the long-term client relationship. Not only do clients expect to converse, but I expect a certain amount of ongoing contact with my clients, building and growing relationships grounded in respect and trust.

Because benefits are a group of individual insurance products, grouped together for the overall benefit of a group of people, linked financially through their employer—due to all of those variables, problems constantly occur, and working with someone who will work with the company to synthesize information to achieve a benefit program employees will value and appreciate is paramount.

May we never return to the days where the salesman was seen only once.

I look forward to continuing to service your needs as they arise.

LIVING ON AN ISLAND

If you can indulge me for a moment, picture an island in the Pacific during World War II. The rugged coastline extends nearly sixteen hundred miles, with a major mountain range cutting through the centre. At least three countries claimed strongholds on this island—the Netherlands, England, the United States—plus at times, depending on battles won or lost, Japan and Germany.

Due to the mountains, mangrove swamps and dense jungle, passage overland is nearly impossible, so it's left untouched. Rainfall runs as high as three hundred inches per year. As one veteran recalled, "It rains daily for nine months, and then the monsoon starts." There are no roads or railways, yet this is the second-largest island in the world. Planes seldom flew over the centre of the island due to dense cloud cover and frequent crashes when attempted.

There is only one recorded plane rescue due the war.

And this is how, right in the heart of this island, an isolated tribe of about 120,000 previously uncontacted people were discovered. They existed as though they were in the Stone Age. They had no notion of even the ocean that surrounded them or the many countries who fought for the territory because they couldn't venture out, and no one could get in. As far as they were concerned, there was no war. They were the Biami people of Papua New Guinea.

In having a group benefit plan, it is easy to claim our territory and accept the status quo—not ask questions or expect more. Before long, we find the benefits to be archaic at best, in the stone age of coverage. Then employees are complaining, wondering what they are contributing to, and the corporation wonders why they even bother.

This is where a second opinion may be a welcome respite from the everyday—to get to know the potential of the wide world of benefits and benefit options; have someone listen to the needs and wants of the company; understand the core values and business practices and only then design and develop a plan to scale the mountainous terrain of achieving the corporate goals.

WHAT YOU DON'T KNOW

Fact: You Simply Don't Know What You Don't Know

That is why we treat every renewal as an opportunity to earn the business all over again. The renewal provides an opportunity to analyze and conduct a thorough review of the insurance or benefit provider's underwriting methods to ensure their basis for establishing the renewal rates is rational and in line with marketplace standards. Where appropriate negotiations are initiated to secure a fair renewal based on current plan design, applicable experience results and insured employee demographics.

Insured Pooled Benefits

The insured pooled benefits are underwritten and administered through an insurance underwriter. When these benefits are referred to as "pooled," it means the carrier blends your plan results with other policyholders for the purpose of assessing premiums and claims experience. Pricing of the pooled benefits is not typically impacted by your experience unless the plan results are significantly above the statistical norm.

Benefits that fall under this category are life insurance, accidental death and dismemberment, dependent life, critical illness and long-term disability.

Pooling these categories of insurance is the most economical approach to pricing this type of benefit because the claims are typically for large amounts, infrequent and difficult to predict. Pooling simply moves the entire risk for experience results to the insured carrier. The factors that most impact the development of the pooled benefit rate are the employee demographics (age, gender and occupation), including the following:

- average age of the group's members as a whole
- how many current employees are insured under the plan
- change in the number of covered employees since last year
- insured experience-rated benefits

Experience-rated benefits under an insured plan are underwritten and administered through an underwriter. These benefits are priced based, to a certain degree, on a company's own usage of these benefits. While a good loss ratio will contribute to a favourable renewal, additional cost factors must also be considered when calculating renewal rates. These factors can include the following:

i. Inflation
ii. Provincial cost downloading and funding changes
iii. Canada's aging workforce
iv. A rise in the volume and cost of prescription drug expenditures
v. Newer, more complex and more expensive treatments and services
vi. Dental fee guides
vii. The IBNR

Self-Insured Benefits

The self-insured benefits, administrative services only (ASO) and health-care spending accounts (HSA) can be provided and administered through an insurance underwriter under the same umbrella as the insured benefits or provided through a separate benefit company. These benefits are funded 100 percent by company corporate dollars where an administration fee is paid based on usage only. There is no payroll deduction to the employee for these benefits. Cost sharing is designed in the copayment—the pay-at-the-counter portion of the plan.

COST SHARING

Options for Splitting the Costs

The means of funding the benefit program should be done in the most effective and efficient manner. There are a number of areas you should review in terms of tax implications, employee participation and management of expenses.

Tax Implications

The chart on the following page illustrates the favorable tax treatment available to corporations versus individuals with respect to premiums. We have demonstrated the impact of funding on the payment of a benefit through the plan.

Having employees use after-tax dollars to fund premiums is a much more expensive route to follow when a company is able to utilize pretax income to pay for benefits. The only employee-paid premiums that deliver any tax benefit are long-term disability and life insurance. Other than these areas, it is clearly more efficient to have the company fund the plan.

Employee Participation

Changes to the cost-sharing arrangement may favorably impact the employee's participation in your plan. Appropriate participation means adequate sharing of risk, which will lead to a more manageable plan for the future. The risk of anti-selection is minimized as well.

Managed Control

Today, employers are expected to provide health and dental plans, which are rising in cost (according to some estimates) at a rate of 10 percent to 15 percent per year. For most companies, this is simply not supportable long term. Employers are now looking to their advisers to provide creative solutions to manage these costs.

An employee-funded program results in an employee-controlled program. Economic reality requires some difficult decisions. The time-consuming and personalized involvement of employees will make appropriate management of the plan virtually impossible.

In order to ensure continued delivery of a fair and comprehensive benefits program, corporate management is critical.

Section 9

Just 'Cause

THE VACATION

"A change is as good as a rest," my mom was fond of saying. Though I didn't exactly know what that meant growing up, as I got older and into my career routine, I came to understand the importance of that advice.

Growing up we were never a family who could afford to go on vacation, but that didn't mean we didn't enjoy holiday time, the benefits or the break from the day-to-day even while enjoying a staycation, whether catching up on chores, finally reading that book, taking a stab at completing a fun project or making memories was the ultimate goal. This is because holidays are necessary for everyone to get rest and refreshment. Some may say they are a lifeline to sanity, a chance to step away from everyday life and reconnect with the people, relax, regroup. In my opinion, they'd be right.

Amazingly, a recent report claims unused holiday days are at a 40-year high, with nearly a quarter of all paid vacation days in the United States not being used, and the United Kingdom is not far behind.

For those who scoff at vacations, be aware that chronic stress takes its toll in part on our body's ability to resist infection, maintain vital functions and even avoid injury. This leads to lack of sleep and the inability to properly digest food, which then may lead the genetic material in the body's cells to become altered. Mentally, people become more irritable, depressed and anxious, and this in turn impacts memory, which may lead to poor decisions.

So whatever the plan—vacation or staycation—take a holiday.

1. **Reduce stress.**
   In the midst of work pressures, it's hard to see things clearly or rationally. Taking a proper break gives perspective, creating a work-life balance.

2. **Improve concentration.**
   Improve effectiveness and concentration by unwinding from the everyday stresses and giving the body the chance to replenish.
3. **Increase satisfaction.**
   Personal time allows people to value themselves, which can lead to better teamwork and boost morale.
4. **Pay attention to family matters.**
   Family time is work and often exhausting. A break allows for time to bond, relax and grow as a family.
5. **Improve physical and mental health.**
   The *New York Times* reported those who take less than one holiday every two years are more likely to suffer from depression and burnout. Those who fail to take annual holidays have a 21 percent higher risk of death from all causes and are 32 percent more likely to die of a heart attack.

So plan ahead, do some research, take the time and, most importantly, don't feel guilty about it!

'TWAS THE WEEK BEFORE PAYROLL

Benefit Poetry

'Twas the week before payroll,
'Twas the week before payroll, when all through the office,
Not an employee sat quiet. It felt like a riot.
Benefit deductions were the source of unrest.
"We're paying too much. Our plan isn't the best!"
"What's this I hear?" the owner said with a hand to his ear.
"Unhappy with benefits at this time of year?"
"Yes!" cried all with shouts from their belly.
"With a second opinion, we could save plenty."
"But who would we call?" the owner asked, quite perplexed.
"Where do we start?" He didn't know what to do next.
"Call MP Benefits," the controller said with a smile.
"They'll treat us just right and do it with style.
With a reputation for fairness and rates unmatched, they're the company for us, and we're unattached."
With a log in to LinkedIn, the controller connected;
in no way throughout the process did he feel neglected.
Plan design analyzed and rates scrutinized,
within the month their fears were neutralized.
And laying the pen next to the contract, the owner rose to shake hands with his new benefit broker, who's also good with the prose.

Saving money's important but still second best
To the service and personal attention, which puts all grievance at rest.
Give us a call today at your leisure;
we'll be happy you did. Business with you would be our pleasure.

ABOUT THE AUTHOR

Lori Power is a business owner, author, and public speaker who believes any job worth doing is worth doing well. As a benefit specialist, she strives to ensure her clients have the best employee group benefit plans possible with options custom designed to suit their needs. She is a board member of Advocis and a member of the Canadian Group Insurance Brokers, the Human Resource Institute of Alberta, and the Canadian Association of Life Underwriters.